Nail it Marketing:

How to Become the #1 Contractor in Your Area

Lori Werner and Sherry Sbraccia

Nail it Marketing: How to Become the #1 Contractor in Your Area
Copyright © 2024 by Lori Werner - Sherry Sbraccia

All rights reserved. No part of this book may be reproduced or transmitted in any form or by any means, electronic or mechanical, including photocopying, recording, or by any information storage and retrieval system, without permission in writing from the author.

Cover design by Sherry Sbraccia
Interior design and typesetting by Sherry Sbraccia

ISBN: 9798328919333
Printed in the United States of America

There is no guarantee associated with the contents of the book. Results will vary and we are not held liable for any damages directly or indirectly as a result of the material.

Dear Reader,

We are excited to present "Nail It Marketing: How to Become the #1 Contractor in Your Area," and we're glad that you've chosen to embark on this marketing journey with us!

We understand the unique challenges and opportunities that come with running a contractor business, from plumbing and electrical work to roofing and handyman services. We have pooled our knowledge to provide you with practical strategies and actionable tips to help you attract more customers and stand out in your local market.

Whether you're just starting your contractor business or aiming to elevate it to new heights, this book is an essential read. We hope you enjoy discovering these insights as much as we enjoyed compiling them.

Sincerely,

Lori Werner

Sherry Sbraccia

Co-Founders of Nail It Marketing Pros

Introduction: The Power of Contractor Marketing

In today's ever-evolving home improvement industry, your role as a contractor is more crucial than ever. As a skilled professional, you have a unique opportunity not only to enhance the homes of your customers but also to establish yourself as the go-to home pro in your community.

In this book, explorethe strategic and practical aspects of Contractor Marketing. We will dive into the art of identifying your ideal customerele, building trust through showcasing your credentials, awards, and certifications, and employing customer-focused marketing strategies.

Each chapter is crafted to equip you with actionable insights and proven strategies, empowering you to rise above the competition and claim your position as the #1 contractor in your area.

Are you ready to transform your business and make a lasting impact in the world of home construction? Let's begin the adventure of becoming the preferred choice for homeowners seeking skilled and reliable contractors. This book is not just about high-level strategies; it's about providing you with specific, implementable actions to distinguish yourself in the competitive construction landscape. Are you ready to unlock the secrets that will push your business to new heights? Let's go!

Allow us to introduce the dynamic duo behind "Contractor Marketing:

How to Become the #1 Contractor in Your Area" by Lori Werner and Sherry Sbraccia, Founders of Nail It Marketing Pros.

Lori Werner and Sherry Sbraccia, a formidable team at Nail It Marekting Pros, are the driving force behind this comprehensive guide. With Lori's founding vision and Sherry's strategic prowess, they bring their collective insights into driving you to become the #1 contractor in your area. Together, they boast over 20 years of combined experience in marketing, dedicating themselves to assisting business owners in navigating the complexities of digital markerting.

Their collaboration ensures that the content is not only insightful but also actionable, drawing from their profound understanding of marketing strategies. Their commitment to staying ahead of the marketing curve is reflected in the strategies presented in this book.

As a team, Lori and Sherry are committed to delivering valuable content that will guide you on your journey to becoming the top contractor in your area. Get ready to benefit from their collaborative wisdom and experience as you read ahead.

Contractor Marketing:

How to Become the #1 Contractor in Your Area

Table of Contents

Chapter 1:   Laying the Foundation of Successful Marketing

Chapter 2:   Evaluating and Transforming Your Marketing Approach

Chapter 3:   How Homeowners Choose a Contractor

Chapter 4:   Your Website: Position Yourself as the Pro

Chapter 5:   Local SEO: Understanding the Elements

Chapter 6:   Your Online Reputation & Why It Matters

Chapter 7:   Overview of Paid Online Advertising Opportunities

Chapter 8:   Pay-Per-Click for Home Services Contractors

Chapter 9:   Paid Online Directories - Which Ones Should You Consider?

Chapter 10: Social Media Mastery

Chapter 11: Email Marketing to Connect With Your Customers

Chapter 12: Leveraging Awards to Position Yourself as the #1 Contractor in Your Area

Chapter 13: Your Journey to Becoming the #1 Contractor

Bonus Material

FREE! Ranking Report & SEO Review

MARKETING REPORT

- » Complete SEO Analysis
- » Ranking Report
- » Citations & Listings Audit
- » Website SEO Scan
- » Conversion Effectiveness
- » Analysis of Social Presence

SCAN THE QR CODE

Chapter 1
Unveiling the Foundations of Successful Marketing

Welcome to the journey of discovering what it takes to maximize your business and take it to the next level. In this chapter, we'll unravel the four key secrets that will pave the way for you to become the #1 contractor in your area.

Before jumping into the secrets, let's lay the groundwork by emphasizing the importance of leveraging all the things that make you the best choice for a homeowner to hire.

Having the best training, equipment, and products is commendable, but it's not enough for people to choose you as their contractor. Homeowners have to see you as the expert for their particular need. They need to view you as someone with the experience, authority, and credibility to solve their need or want..

Homeowners take time to pick the right contractor, especially when looking at high-ticket services. Personally, I can attest to this reality, having had to research contractors to repair storm damage. The first thing I did was Google "best contractor in my area."

Unveiling the Foundations of Successful Marketing

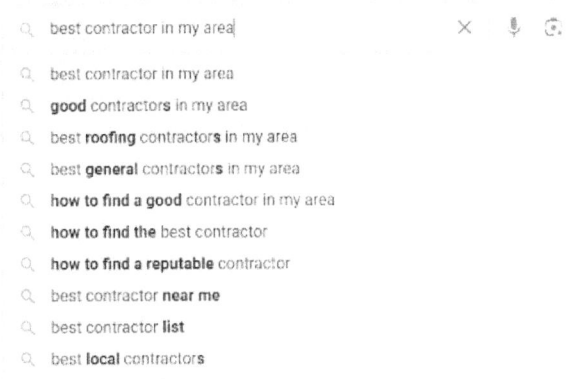

From there I looked at the "3-pack", those are the contractors that show up in that little box by the map:

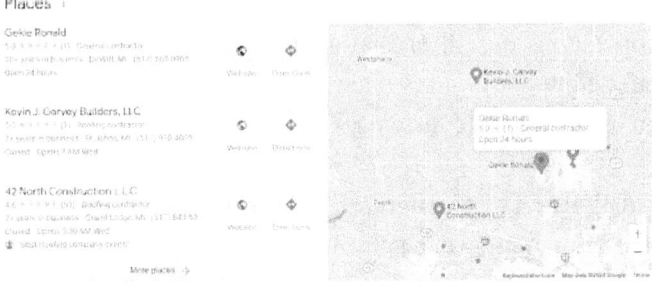

After that, I'm looking at the reviews to see if there were any negative experiences and what those are as well as reading the positive feedback. After I look at the reviews, I'm visiting their website to see what services they offer and if it fits my needs. As you can see there are many steps a homeowner takes before they decide to pick up that phone and give you a call.

It wasn't an instantaneous decision, but rather a carefully researched one.

This story underscores the importance of making your services visible to potential customers and ensuring that your reviews and website are high-quality and up-to-date. People actively seek solutions to their home needs and wants, but the challenge lies in making them aware that you offer the services they're looking for.

Furthermore, it's crucial to acknowledge the competitive landscape of contractors. Numerous contractors offer similar services, making it necessary for you to stand out. As we dig into this book's four secrets of contractor marketing, remember that your investment in time, training, and technology equips you with the skills and desire to make a significant impact.

Marketing Starts from Within
Before we embark on the expansive journey of marketing strategies, it's essential to lay a solid foundation with a core principle: effective marketing starts from within. YYour business is not just a site where home improvement projects are completed for customers; it is a dynamic ecosystem driven by your team's skill, dedication, and enthusiasm.

The professionalism of your staff, the quality of work, and the efficiency of your operations are all crucial elements of the customer experience. Therefore, before diving into external marketing strategies, we must first transform our offices into thriving, welcoming hubs.

Quality of Work: The Cornerstone of Your Reputation
No amount of marketing can substitute for poor workmanship. Quality of work and quality control are fundamental to your success as a contractor. Homeowners talk, and word-of-mouth is a powerful marketing tool. When you consistently deliver high-quality work, your reputation will precede you, leading to more referrals and repeat business. Here are some steps to ensure top-notch quality:

1. **Set High Standards**: Clearly define and communicate the quality standards you expect from your team. Regularly review and reinforce these standards to ensure everyone is aligned.
2. **Quality Control Processes:** Implement rigorous quality control checks at every stage of a project. This includes initial inspections, ongoing checks during the project, and a final review before handing

over the project to the homeowner.
3. **Continuous Training:** Invest in ongoing training for your team to keep them updated on the latest techniques, materials, and industry standards. A well-trained team is equipped to deliver high-quality work consistently.
4. **Customer Feedback:** Encourage homeowners to provide feedback after project completion. Use this feedback to make improvements and address any issues promptly. Positive feedback can also be used as testimonials on your website and marketing materials.

Hiring Your A-Team

Your team is not just a group of professionals; they are ambassadors for your business. Each team member, from the office staff to the construction crew, contributes to the reputation that customers remember. A well-chosen, trained, and motivated team can turn your business into a magnet for customer loyalty and positive word-of-mouth marketing.

Motivating your team members and maintaining their motivation can be a significant challenge. However, it is critical to running any successful business and should not be overlooked. Motivation directly impacts job performance. Motivated individuals and teams achieve personal, group, and overall business goals. Moreover, motivated individuals who consistently deliver high-quality work are more likely to overcome obstacles, tackle challenges, and use their time productively.

Motivating your team requires effective, dynamic leadership, which is not something you do "to" your team, but something you do "with" them. Some keys to effective leadership include:

- **Integrity:** Leading with integrity by modeling the behavior you want others to display. Setting clearly communicated and measurable standards and then training, coaching, and motivating those standards maintain a culture of integrity. Leading with integrity builds trust. Show the staff that you trust them by creating a culture of self-responsibility; encourage them to solve problems, contribute to building the business, and organize and implement new ways to handle day-to-day

challenges.
- **Partnership:** Build relationships with your crew by sharing the big picture and by positively emphasizing the importance of their role in achieving it. Coaching helps to build partnerships. This is not about discipline; it is about encouraging your crew and staff to discover their best and perform at it. One way for a staff member to contribute to the big picture is to develop and grow. Ask staff or crew members to stretch beyond what you have observed them doing in the past and provide them with opportunities for growth with advanced education, training, and special projects.
- **Affirmation:** Observe the good in your staff and crew and offer praise and affirmation. Reward the team for their contributions. Learn what staff members feel positive about doing and maximize their opportunity to contribute in those areas. Create opportunities to communicate with your staff and crew members.
- **Rewards and Incentives:** For a rewards and incentives program to be effective, clear and measurable performance goals must be set. These goals must also be clearly communicated with the team with details such as the time period within which the goal should be achieved, and how the goal will be measured. This could include solving a problem that results in a new best practice. Lastly, and most importantly, ongoing encouragement, motivation, and coaching (as needed) should be provided to support the crew in goal achievement. Rewards for achieving goals, contributing new ideas, or for solving problems is a great way to keep the crew motivated. One way to reward your staff is to offer Free Lunch Friday. This is a terrific incentive and it allows your crew to feel appreciated and that they are more than a number. Take the time to understand what would be a good incentive for each individual in your office. Of course, you can't diminish the importance of showing employee appreciation. Acknowledging excellent performance is best done with a sincere "thank you." You might send a personal note or send a text acknowledging their great work.

Meetings:
Regular meetings are important in developing and maintaining staff motivation. In busy contractor offices, it is often difficult to find time to com-

municate new information or to feel "connected" to the team. Meetings provide this opportunity and allow for the staff to communicate with you and with each other without the distraction of the bustling business.

Meetings can be used in many ways. Every meeting does not have to have the same purpose or agenda, and they can be used for a number of reasons including:

- To update the staff on changes in the business and to communicate new information.
- To address and solve a problem.
- To celebrate a recent success.
- To plan an upcoming event.
- To conduct a training.
- To demonstrate a new or existing product or technology.
- To review and refresh existing policies and procedures.

Some tips on conducting a successful meeting include:
- Keep agendas manageable in scope. The entire agenda should be covered during the allocated time.
- Be prepared. Outline the agenda and the goals of the meeting.
- Clearly communicate the date, time, and meeting place in advance to give staff time to plan.
- Assign a "scribe" who will take notes and distribute minutes to the staff.
- Be mindful of maintaining an open forum for comments, questions, and suggestions, while making sure to stay on time and topic. For items that require more time, recommend they be added to an agenda for a future meeting.
- Meetings should be upbeat, relaxed, and comfortable.
- End the meeting on time.
- Have the "scribe" post minutes so that any action items assigned, decisions made, or information dispelled are clearly documented.
- All action items should be put on the next agenda for follow-up.

Crafting the Marketing Environment: Action Items

☐ **Team Evaluation:** Conduct a thorough assessment of your team culture and working environment. Experience your business from a homeowner's perspective. Look up your business online, scrutinize your Google listing, evaluate your website, and call the business incognito. Identify areas for improvement in the online and offline homeowner journey.

☐ **Injecting Fun to the Team:** What is the vibe of your crew? The happiness within your team translates to the job. The attitude of your crew sets the tone for the homeowner experience. A team with a positive attitude is your best marketing asset. Homeowners not only seek contractor expertise but also yearn for a positive, streamlined experience. Make the extra effort to infuse happiness into every interaction, and watch it transform into a powerful marketing tool.
"A team with a great attitude is the best marketing there is"

☐ **Quality Control Assessment:** Regularly review your quality control processes to ensure that the work delivered meets or exceeds industry standards. This includes initial inspections, ongoing project checks, and a final review before project completion.

☐ **Feedback Loop:** Create a system for collecting and acting on feedback from customers. Use this feedback to make continuous improvements in your services and address any issues promptly. Positive feedback can be showcased as testimonials on your website and marketing materials.

☐ **Training and Development:** Invest in ongoing training for your team to keep their skills sharp and up-to-date with the latest industry trends and standards. Encourage them to pursue additional certifications and attend workshops.

- ☐ **Reward Excellence:** Recognize and reward outstanding performance and innovative ideas within your team. This could be through formal recognition programs, bonuses, or other incentives that motivate your team to strive for excellence.

- ☐ **Communication:** Maintain open lines of communication with your team. Regularly update them on company goals, changes, and successes. Encourage them to share their ideas and feedback, fostering a collaborative and inclusive work environment.

- ☐ **Customer Journey Mapping:** Map out the entire customer journey from initial contact to project completion. Identify key touch points and ensure that each interaction is positive and professional. This holistic approach helps in delivering a seamless and satisfying customer experience.

By focusing on these action items, you will create a strong marketing environment that not only attracts new customers but also retains existing ones, ultimately driving your business to greater success.

Chapter 2

Evaluating and Transforming Your Marketing Approach

Let's dig into the common issues contractors might run into and figure out how to handle the shift from old-school to modern marketing methods.

Recognizing Marketing Missteps

Misstep 1: Introducing New Services Without a Confident Marketing Strategy

Embracing new services is a thrilling venture, but without a solid marketing strategy, you risk it just being an idea and wasting money on new equipment to implement that just turns into a dust collector. A contractor invests in new equipment with the hope that it will significantly boost revenue. However, enthusiasm alone doesn't translate into success.

We often witness this cycle: a contractor acquires a new piece of equipment, or has an idea of how to improve their services, believing it will be the key to substantial revenue growth. Unfortunately, the excitement fades when there's no real launch strategy or an effective marketing plan in place.

Before investing in new equipment or extensive crew training, it's crucial to have a solid marketing plan in place. Don't let your valuable investments become overlooked assets. Make sure you have a strategy to inform the community about your new services and technology.

In the upcoming sections, we'll explore strategies to bolster your confidence in marketing new services, ensuring that your investments contribute to the growth and success of your business.

Misstep 2: Past Marketing Attempts that Yielded Disappointing Results

Many contractors find themselves in a frustrating cycle—having invested in marketing initiatives that either failed to deliver results or, worse, turned out to be a rip-off. This disillusionment often stems from experiences with marketing agencies, where contractors may hop from one agency to another without seeing any tangible outcomes.

Some contractors may have worked with agencies claiming local expertise but fall short in understanding the nuances of the local contractor space. Picture an agency marketing not only contractors but also local restaurants, pet groomers, hair stylists and more. Such agencies lack the specialized knowledge required for effective contractor marketing.

This let down can lead contractors to feel they've wasted both time and money. The frustration reaches a point where they think about abandoning marketing efforts altogether, thinking, "to heck with it." It's important to recognize that not all marketing approaches are created equal, and the key lies in partnering with a specialized agency that understands contractor marketing.

In the upcoming sections, we'll dive into insider tips that we implement for our customers ensuring you gain insights tailored to the unique demands of contractor services.

Misstep 3: Overworked Staff with Limited Marketing Expertise

Another common misstep involves relying on staff members to handle your marketing, often on top of their existing responsibilities. Your staff may find themselves wearing multiple hats, such as being a business admin or business manager, all while being tasked with marketing duties. Despite their dedication, they may lack true marketing expertise.

This situation often results in what I like to call "kind-of sort-of marketing." Your amdin may be doing a bit of marketing, but it occurs sporadically, squeezed in between their numerous other responsibilities. The outcome is only partial results, and, in reality, no actual cost savings. In fact, this approach tends to make your staff less efficient in their primary roles.

It's important to recognize that expecting your staff to effectively market your business while juggling a myriad of other responsibilities is an unrealistic demand. In the upcoming sections, we'll discuss strategies to empower your staff and streamline your marketing efforts without compromising their efficiency in their primary roles.

Misstep 4: Increased Operating Expenses, Declining Income

In the world of home contracting, one of the toughest challenges is keeping your expenses in check while trying to maintain or grow your income. It's a tough balance to strike, especially with rising material costs, unexpected repairs, and the constant need for updated equipment and tools. However, marketing plays a crucial role in addressing these challenges and can be a game-changer for your business. By effectively marketing your services, you can attract more customers, justify premium pricing, and ensure a steady flow of projects that keep your cash flow healthy. Here are some common pitfalls and how to tackle them head-on.

Challenges You Might Face and How Marketing Helps:

Rising Material Costs:

The prices for lumber, steel, and other essential materials can fluctuate wildly. When prices go up, your profit margins shrink if you're not careful.

How Marketing Helps:
- *Value Proposition:* Emphasize the quality and reliability of your work in your marketing materials. When customers understand the value they're getting, they're more likely to accept higher prices.

- *Targeting the Right Audience:* Use targeted marketing to reach customers who are willing to pay a premium for high-quality work. Tailoring your message to affluent neighborhoods or high-end renovation projects can help you land more lucrative jobs.

- *Promotions and Deals:* Strategically offer promotions or bundles that can absorb some of the rising costs while still attracting customers.

Labor Costs

Finding skilled labor can be tough, and retaining good workers means competitive wages and benefits. This can eat into your profits if not managed well.

How Marketing Helps:
- *Employer Branding:* Promote your business as a great place to work. Highlight your commitment to fair wages, benefits, and a positive work environment. This can attract skilled labor without necessarily having to outbid competitors.

- *Showcase Expertise:* Use marketing to showcase the expertise and skill of your team. When customers see the quality of your workforce, they're more likely to justify paying higher prices.

- Community Involvement: Engage in community-based marketing efforts. Sponsoring local events or participating in community projects can boost your reputation and attract both customers and potential employees.

Overhead Costs

Office expenses, marketing costs, and administrative fees can creep up and reduce your bottom line.

How Marketing Helps:

- *Digital Marketing:* Utilize cost-effective digital marketing strategies, such as social media, email marketing, and SEO, to reach a broader audience without breaking the bank.

- *Efficient Campaigns:* Track and analyze your marketing campaigns to ensure they're delivering a good return on investment. Focus on the strategies that bring in the most business for the least cost.

- *Online Reviews and Referrals:* Encourage satisfied customers to leave positive reviews and refer others. Word-of-mouth marketing is powerful and virtually free, helping you reduce the need for expensive advertising.

Marketing emerges as the lifeblood of any business. Effectively communicating the value of your services becomes a crucial aspect in sustaining a thriving business.

In the next parts, we'll lay out ways to handle operating costs and show you how marketing can be a game-changer for keeping your business strong. We'll dive into how good money management and smart marketing can work together to keep your business growing for the long haul.

Old School vs. New School Marketing: Navigating the Shifting Terrain
The way you market your business can make or break your success. The methods that worked decades ago just don't cut it in today's digital age. It's crucial to update your marketing tactics to stay competitive and attract new customers. Here, we'll explore the differences between old school and new school marketing and why it's essential for home contractors to get up to date.

Old School Marketing Tactics

Newspaper Ads: Placing ads in local newspapers was a primary way to reach potential customers. In today's climate, newspaper readership is plummeting being replaced with online readership.

Cold Calling: Contractors would call potential customers directly to pitch their services. Today people view this as intrusive and will not answer their phone if it is listed as a potential spam or unlisted phone number. You run the risk of being blocked.

Direct Mail Flyers: Sending postcards or flyers to homes was a common way to advertise. Now most of mail, especially postcards, get thrown away without being read. Email marketing and online ads have become more effective and is environmentally friendly.

New School Marketing Tactics

SEO: The first support of your marketing engine is Local SEO. SEO ensures your business appears at the top of search results when potential customers look for services online. This involves optimizing your Google Business profile to ensure it reflects the comprehensive range of services you offer. When someone searches for a contractor near me" or "roofer near me," your goal is to be the top result. This involves not only being discovered but being chosen. How? By amassing a bunch of 5-star reviews. These reviews not only testify to your excellence but also significantly impact your Google ranking. You will also want to optimize your website with relevant keywords, creating high-quality content, and earning backlinks from reputable sites.

Social Media: Social media is an important tool to engage potential customers where they spend a lot of time. Platforms like Facebook, Instagram, and LinkedIn can showcase your work and interact with customers. To make sure you are utilizing it to it's highest potential, post regularly, use high-quality images and videos your your projects, and engage with followers through comments and messages.

Online Reviews and Testimonials: Online reviews and testimonials build trust and credibility. Positive reviews on platforms like Google, Yelp, and Houzz can significantly influence potential customers. Encourage satisfied customers to leave reviews. It also helps to respond to reviews professionally, and showcase testimonials on your website.

Pay-per-click (PPC) Advertising: PPC allows contractors to target specific demographics, locations, and search terms. This means your ads are shown to people actively searching for contracting services in your area, increasing the likelihood of attracting potential customers. You only pay when someone clicks on your ad, ensuring that your advertising budget is spent on interested prospects. This can be more cost-effective than traditional advertising methods where you pay a fixed amount regardless of results.

Chapter 3

How Homeowners Choose a Contractor

Let's get into the mindset of how homeowners go about choosing a contractor. Word-of-mouth is still king. Most people are going to ask their friends and family, who they recommend. If they move to a new area, they often join a local community forum like Facebook Groups and post that they are looking for a contractor and see who people recommend in the comments. As a home contractor, your aim is to be the resounding recommended business in your area.

In the modern world, even word-of-mouth ends up going online. After a recommendation, homeowners head to Google to research the contractor and to get the phone number or website to learn more.

On Google, they will research the recommended contractor, but also usually look at the top 2-3 others in the area. They read the Google reviews and compare each contractor. They are looking for validation that the recommended company is in fact the right choice and is worth them taking time out of their busy day to have you give an estimate. Reviews become the peak of trust. They are also a huge factor in search ranking on Google.

Simultaneously, homeonwers seek assurance in your expertise and authority. They are looking for a contractor who doesn't just check the boxes but takes a look at the whole project and doesn't miss anything. What does your online presence convey? Is your website all stock photography or does it showcase your expertise, your team, your projects, and credentials?

Next up is the way you communicate. Is your communication style part of your online marketing strategy so potential customers can get to know you and your business? Understanding how homeowners decide isn't just strategy; it's your backstage pass to being not just seen but chosen. In the next section, we're digging into finding your ideal customer—an essential step in making sure your business takes the lead role.

Unveiling Your Ideal Customer Avatar
Alright, let's talk about something crucial: understanding who your ideal homeowners. It's not just about offering services; it's about making sure your marketing connects with the exact homeowner who needs your services most.

Before you unleash your marketing strategy, you need to identify:

WHO your ideal customer is
WHERE they hang out online
WHAT problem are they dealing with

Knowing your ideal customer guides your social media strategy, helping you create posts, videos, and lead magnets that draw in more leads. it also influences your understanding of homeowners' needs, steering you toward new services that cater to those needs.

It helps you craft your offers and promotions, speaking directly to your avatar and motivating them to schedule an estimate. It also boosts your email marketing effectiveness, leading to higher open rates, better conversion rates, and even specific campaigns tailored to different avatars. You'll discover which paid platforms you should run ads on — and what targeting options you should use.

Demographics: The Avatar Blueprint:
Applying demographic information breathes life into your patient avatar. Gender, age range, marital status, age of children, annual household income, education level, radius around your business, target cities, hobbies, and interests—all these elements build a vibrant picture of your ideal homeowner.

These demographic details aren't just for show; they're the backbone of your targeted marketing efforts. Whether you're jumping into Facebook and Instagram Ads or developing a lead magnet, your customer avatar's demographics are your guiding stars.

Example Avatar:
Name: John and Jane Homeowner
Demographics:
- Age: 35-50
- Marital Status: Married
- Children: 2 (ages 8 and 12)
- Occupation: Mid-level professionals (e.g., project manager, teacher)
- Income: $75,000 - $120,000 combined annual income
- Location: Suburban areas
- Homeownership Status: Own a 3-4 bedroom single-family home

Psychographics:
- Values: Quality work, reliability, and trustworthiness in contractors
- Hobbies: Gardening, DIY home projects, family outings
- Goals: To maintain and improve their home's value, create a safe and comfortable environment for their family
- Challenges: Lack of time for home maintenance and repairs, difficulty finding trustworthy and skilled contractors, budget constraints

Behavior:
- Internet Usage: Regularly use the internet for researching home improvement ideas, reading reviews, and finding local services
- Social Media: Active on Facebook, Instagram, and Pinterest for home inspiration

- Shopping Habits: Prefer local businesses, rely heavily on online reviews and recommendations from friends and family

Pain Points:
- Concerns about costs and hidden fees in contracting work
- Worry about the quality and reliability of contractors
- Limited time to oversee home improvement projects
- Previous negative experiences with contractors

Ideal Contractor:
- Reliable and punctual
- Transparent pricing with no hidden fees
- High-quality workmanship
- Strong online presence with positive reviews
- Good communication skills and easy-to-reach

Marketing Messaging:
- "Transform your home with quality you can trust."
- "Reliable, affordable, and hassle-free home improvements."
- "Let us handle your home projects so you can focus on what matters most."
- "Check out our rave reviews from homeowners just like you."

By creating this detailed homeowner avatar, contractors can better tailor their marketing efforts to address the specific needs and preferences of their ideal customers, leading to more effective and targeted campaigns.

Chapter 4
Your Website - Position Yourself as the Pro

Your website stands as the virtual gateway to your business, a powerful tool to establish credibility, foster trust, and engage with your target audience effectively. Tailoring your website to the specific needs of homeowners requires careful consideration of both structure and content. Beyond the fundamental pages, this chapter looks into essential elements that can elevate your online presence.

So, what pages should your website have? What navigation structure should you create? These are the core pages.

- Home
- About Us
- Our Services
- Service Area
- Online Specials or Coupons
- Before and After sections or a Work Showcase
- Reviews and Testimonials
- Blog or Resources
- Contact Us
- FAQ Page
- Careers or Employment Opportunities

Additional features should include Social Media Links and newsletter signup for specials and promotions.

By including these pages and features, you can enhance your website's visibility, improve user experience, and increase your chances of converting visitors into customers. Your website needs to be a clear description of who you are as a company or individual business owner.

A visitor who stumbles upon your website shouldn't have to do a thorough investigation to figure out who you are and what exactly you do. This means it's important to clearly mention your business name and sum up your services above the fold section of your website. A clear and specific description will attract the visitor's attention immediately - within two to three seconds - and encourage them to spend time on your website.

Customer Testimonials
Ensure you have a direct link driving visitors to your online reviews and testimonials, as discussed previously. Incorporate a testimonials section on your homepage that dynamically updates with the latest reviews. This keeps your content fresh and relevant.

Pro Tip: Feature video testimonials from satisfied customers. Video content is highly engaging and can significantly boost trust and credibility.
You should also prominently display your credentials, such as BBB accreditation or membership in the local chamber of commerce or industry association, either in the sidebar or in the header graphic. This reassures potential customers of your credibility and community involvement, making them more comfortable doing business with you. More on how to get awards later in this book!

Make sure your company name, address, and phone number (NAP) are on every page of your website. While listing your address on each page may not be critical for customer decision-making, NAP consistency is vital for

Google Maps optimization and local SEO rankings
The footer section is an ideal place to include this information, ensuring it appears on all pages, including the Contact Us page.

Pro Tip: Utilize schema markup, also known as structured data which is a form of microdata that you can add to your website's HTML to improve the way search engines read and represent your page in search results. It helps search engines understand the content on your site and provides more informative results to users for your NAP information to enhance local SEO and improve your chances of appearing in local search results.

Authentic Images
Infuse personality into your website with authentic photos and videos. Showcase your company by featuring yourself, the business owner, and the people who work in the business: the office team, technicians, etc. Highlight the office, trucks, and equipment you use. Authentic imagery builds trust and allows visitors to get to know you before they even pick up the phone.

Pro Tip: Incorporate a "Meet the Team" section with short bios and photos or videos of each team member. This personal touch can make a significant difference in building a connection with potential clients.

Consider this scenario: a potential customer visits two different sites for similar services. One site uses generic images, while the other features genuine pictures of the actual team and equipment. The authentic site will convert visitors at a much higher rate. Let your real personality shine through on your website.

Craft messaging that explains why they should choose your company
Highlight your unique selling points (USPs) and what sets you apart from the competition. Guide visitors through a journey where they learn why you are the best option, showcasing your online reviews and special offers to drive immediate action.

Pro Tip: Use a combination of text, images, and short video clips to explain your USPs. Video content is particularly effective for capturing attention and conveying information quickly.

Pro Tip: Implement interactive elements like a chatbot or live chat feature to engage visitors and answer their questions in real-time, increasing the chances of converting them into customers.

Make Sure Your Website is Mobile Responsive
Cater to the growing number of users accessing websites via smartphones by ensuring a condensed, mobile-ready version of your site, facilitating easy navigation and contact.

How to Ensure That Your Website Converts Visitors into Leads
This next section focuses on website conversion fundamentals, emphasizing how to set up your website, the messaging on your website, and the navigational flow to ensure maximum conversion and profitability from your entire online marketing effort.

No matter how effective your Pay Per Click campaigns or search engine optimization efforts are, if your website isn't set up in a compelling way for users, it won't give them a reason to choose you over the competition.

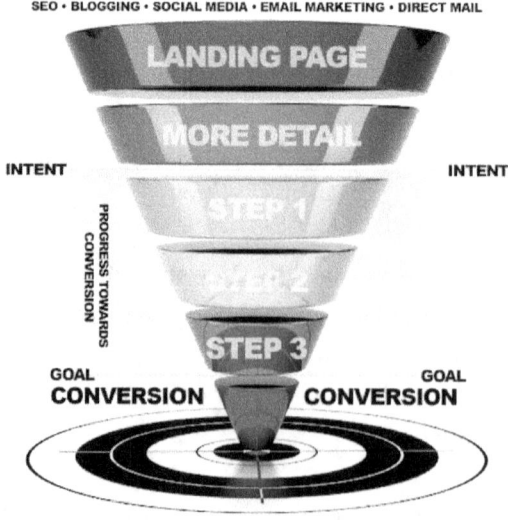

Here's how to make sure your website converts visitors into leads:

Conversion Fundamentals

Be Real

1. People resonate with real individuals. Avoid stock photography and showcase authentic images of your team, office, and equipment. Display pictures of the owner, the team, your office, and your service vehicles. This approach helps potential customers feel they are dealing with real people, which is crucial in the home services industry.

Compelling Messaging

2. Your website content should draw visitors in and make them connect with your business. For example, your homepage should have a strong, trust-building message like, "Looking for a trustworthy and reliable [roofer/plumber/handyman/electrician]? You've come to the right place. We've been operating with trust, innovation, and excellence for over 30 years."

Clear Call to Action

3. Every page should have a clear call to action (CTA). For instance, "Call us now for immediate service" or "Click here for special offers and discounts." This encourages visitors to take action rather than continue browsing.

Address Specific Concerns

4. Tailor your messaging to address the specific concerns of your potential customers. For example, on a plumbing services page, you might write, "Dealing with a leaky faucet? Call our experienced team for prompt and reliable plumbing services." Include a CTA after every block of text.

Interactive Elements

5. Include interactive elements like web forms on each page, or at the very least, on your Contact Us page. This ensures that if visitors are not inclined to call, they can still provide their information for you to contact them. Your phone number should be

prominently displayed in the top right-hand corner of every page.

Utilize Reviews and Testimonials

6. Use reviews, testimonials, and videos to build trust. Create simple videos for each service page explaining why your business is the best choice. Provide external proof by linking to review sites like Angi's List and Google Maps, where potential customers can see testimonials from other satisfied clients.

Example of How to Structure A High-Converting Home Services Website

Above the Fold Section

- Company Logo: Place your logo in the top left-hand corner, but don't make it too large.
- Phone Number: Display your phone number prominently in the top right-hand corner.
- Professional Photos: Use professionally shot photos of your team and work environment. Authentic, welcoming images can significantly improve the user experience and trust.
- Engaging Headlines and Bullet Points: Use attention-grabbing headlines and bullet points to highlight your services.
- Calls to Action: Include clear CTAs like "Contact Us for a Free Quote" or "Schedule Your Service Today."

Main Navigation

- Ease of Use: Ensure your main navigation is easy to find and descriptive. Guide users through your site with clear pathways to relevant information.
- Contact Forms: Place a contact form above the fold to capture leads.

Get to the Point

- Introduction: The first paragraph should briefly introduce who you are and what you do.
- Detailed Information: Provide more detailed information on internal pages like the About Us page.

Interactive Features
- Sliders: Use slider graphics for visual appeal and to highlight key services.
- Social Media Integration: Include social media icons to showcase another side of your company and improve your SEO.

Content Updates and SEO
- Blog: Maintain a blog with regular updates to provide useful information and improve your search engine rankings.
- Latest News: Include a Latest News section with press releases to keep content fresh and relevant.

In essence, your website serves as a dynamic tool to not only inform but also impress potential customers, positioning you as a top-tier contractor in your specialty. By incorporating these elements, you can create a robust online presence that resonates with authenticity, expertise, and values.

Chapter 5
Local SEO: Understanding the Elements

Let's get into the nitty-gritty of local search engine optimization (SEO) — your ticket to being the top choice in your community for home improvement work. We're breaking it down into the Google Business profile, online listings, and the golden nugget—your online reputation.

Local SEO, or search engine optimization, is your key to getting noticed in your community. Imagine it as your digital billboard attracting homeowners in your area. Getting listed on the first page of Google for "Your City + Specialty" comes down to four primary factors:

- Having a claimed and verified Google Business Profile Listing
- Having an optimized Google Business Profile for your local area
- Having a consistent N.A.P. (Name, Address, Phone Number Profile) across the web so that Google feels confident that you are a legitimate organization located in the place you have listed and serving the market you claim to serve.
- Having reviews from your previous customers in your service area

If you have each of these four factors working in your favor you will **SIGNIFICANTLY** improve the probability of ranking on page one of Google in your market.

How to Establish a Strong Name, Address, Phone Number Profile

One crucial element of your local SEO is maintaining a consistent Name, Address, and Phone Number (N.A.P.) profile across the web, especially for optimizing your ranking on Google Business.

Google recognizes a consistent N.A.P. as a signal of authority, making it important for every business to establish a strong foundation. Before getting into claiming your Google Business Profile and building out your other online directory listings, start by defining your authentic N.A.P. Make certain that it is uniformly referenced across various online platforms.

Consistency, in this context, means always using the legitimate name of your business. For instance, if your Business is "John's Home Service," consistently list it as such, avoiding variations like "John's Services". Be cautious of misinformation suggesting keyword stuffing in your business name. Keyword stuffing refers to the practice of loading a webpage with excessive keywords or phrases in an attempt to manipulate a site's ranking in search engine results. Some examples include Repeating the same words or phrases so frequently that it sounds unnatural. For example, "We offer the best roofing services. Our roofing services are top-rated. Contact us for roofing services today." While it may have been effective in the past, it now violates Google's policies. Google can penalize sites that engage in keyword stuffing by lowering their rankings or removing them from search results altogether.

Modern SEO approaches uses related keywords and synonyms to provide context and avoid over-reliance on a single keyword. By focusing on user experience and providing valuable, relevant content, websites can improve their SEO without resorting to keyword stuffing.

Maintain uniformity across all directory sources by listing your exact company name, using the same primary business phone number, and presenting your address consistently. Avoid the temptation to assign unique phone numbers to each directory; this only confuses your online profile.

When it comes to directory listings, utilize your primary phone number, the original business name, and the principal address consistently. For instance, if your business is situated at "1367 South West 87th Street, Suite Number 105," ensure it is listed exactly the same way on every platform.

Pay attention to the finer details to achieve a seamless name/address profile across the web. Avoid inconsistencies like using "South West" in one place and "SW" in another. Precision is key.

To discern your N.A.P. from Google's perspective, conduct a search for "Your Business" and analyze the references on Google Maps. Compare this with high-authority sites like YP.com, Yelp.com, and Angi'es List. Identify the prevalent combination of N.A.P. and adopt it consistently for all future directory work.

Remember, in the world of contractors, attention to detail and a cohesive online identity can be the key to attracting the right homeowners and establishing your business as a trusted authority.

Next, we are going to unlock the full potential of your business with the Google Business Profile— a powerful and FREE tool that enhances your online presence, engages potential customers, and boosts your visibility in local searches.

Google Business Profile (GBP):
When someone in your community is searching for a contractor —let's say they need a roofer, or an electrician—93% of the time, they will click on one of the top three listings that pop up on Google, referred to as the "3-Pack". Think of it like this: imagine you're craving pizza and you search for "pizza near me." You're likely to choose from the first three pizza places that show up, right? It's the same for homeowners looking for contractor services.

For you, as home contractor, this means that securing a spot in the Google 3-Pack is like having a backstage pass to homeowner choices. Homeowners are highly likely to contact and choose a contractor from this exclusive trio. So, when your business shines in that top three, you're not just visible—you're the go-to choice for people in your area. It's not just crucial; it's the golden ticket to being their preferred place.

Getting into the Google 3-Pack involves optimizing your online presence, specifically your Google Business profile. Here are key steps to increase your chances of securing a spot:

Claim and Optimize Your Google Business Profile:
Below you will find a step-by-step guide for checking, claiming and managing your Local Business Listings on Google.

1. Go to https://www.google.com/business/

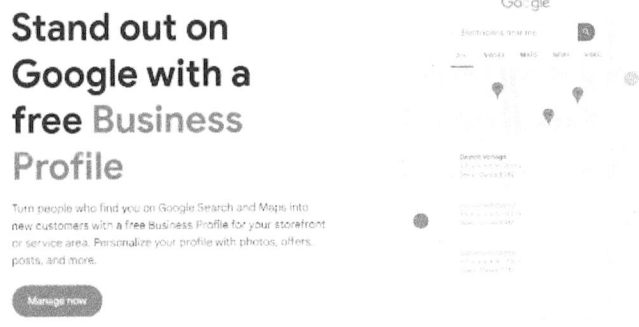

2. Claim your business

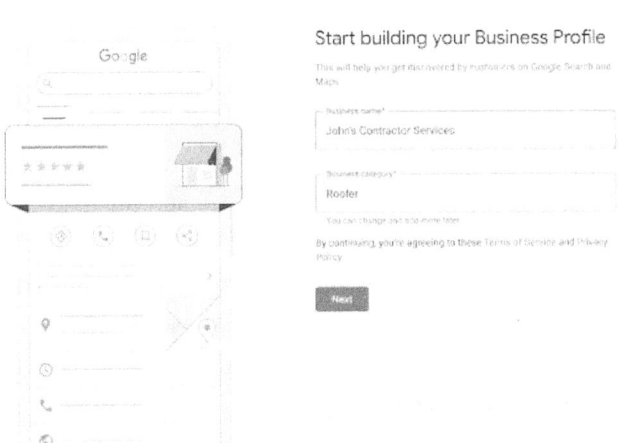

3. Enter your business address and all pertinent information

4. Choose a verification method
- By postcard
- By phone
- By email
- Instant verification

5. Once your listings are claimed, go to your Google Business Profile Dashboard and fill in all the necessary information to optimize your profile.

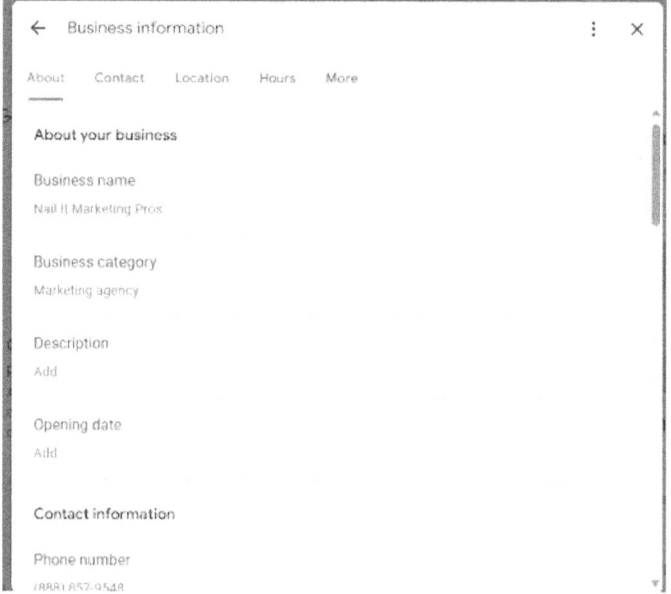

Update Your Company Name to Read "Company Name"
e.g. John's Contractor Services - Don't add any additional keywords here.

Add Your Website Address - This will create an important inbound link

Add a Detailed Business Description
This should highlight your services and specialties, and what sets your

business apart. Be sure to write the description in a friendly language, avoiding contractor jargon. Naturally incorporate local keywords in your description to enhance local search visibility.

Next, Choose Primary and Secondary Categories
These should accurately represent your services. Consider the specific specialties you offer within contracting such as plumber, Roofing Contractor, electrician, concrete contractor, painter, woodworker, dry wall contractor, and more. You will choose one primary category and can add up to 9 secondary categories. Although you are allowed to add 9 secondary, we suggest keeping it to around 3 or 4. If you add more, it can confuse Google and dilute your ability to rank in your primary category. For example if you are a roofing contractor the secondary categories you could include are:

1. Roofing Contractor
2. Gutter Contractor
3. Siding Contractor
4. Roofing Supply Store
5. Roofing Consultant
6. Roofing Materials Supplier
7. Roofing Repair Service

List Your Core Services and Products
Clearly outline the primary services you offer, such as Roofing Contractor, woodworker, and plumber, and be sure to specify any unique or specialized services that distinguish your business. If applicable, feature products related to your industry, such as roofing materials used or if you have any high-tech tools being used that set you a part from the competition, and clearly describe the benefits of each product. Don't forget to incorporate keywords in your descriptions to enhance local search visibility.

Business Hours
Double-check that your business hours are accurate, including any variations for specific days or services. Update hours promptly for holidays or special occasions when the office may be closed.

Phone Number

Use a local number (not an 800 number), and make sure it is your real office number rather than a tracking number. We find that 800 numbers don't rank well. If you use a tracking number, it won't be consistent with your other online directory listings and will result in poor ranking.

Upload PHOTOS – AS MANY AS POSSIBLE

Google values businesses that provide a rich and informative experience for users, and an extensive collection of high-quality photos contributes significantly to this. A study conducted by Google found that businesses with photos receive 42% more requests for directions and 35% more click-throughs to their websites. This data underscores the impact of visual content on user engagement. Google's algorithm interprets a robust gallery of photos as a positive signal, signaling to the search engine that your business is active, reputable, and deserving of higher visibility. Therefore, regularly updating and diversifying your photo library not only enhances the user experience but also positively influences your position in local search results.

Add high-quality images that reflect your services. Feature images that highlight your team's expertise and quality services. Consider, including photos and brief bios of key team members, fostering a personal connection with homeowners.

You can also create geo context for the photos by uploading them to a video-sharing site like Panoramio.com (a Google Property) that enables you to Geotag your photos to your company's location.

Videos

Upload VIDEOS. They don't have to be professionally produced and will resonate well with your potential customers. A best practice is to upload the videos to YouTube and then Geotag them using the advanced settings.

Leveraging your Google Business Profile as a platform for educational content is a strategic move that can significantly benefit businesses in the contractor space. By incorporating informative videos within your profile, you have the opportunity to directly engage with potential customers and showcase your expertise.

Consider creating videos that touch on common homeowner issues. Here are 20 ideas to get you started:

Home Maintenance Tips:
- Discuss regular maintenance tasks to prolong the life of various home components (e.g., plumbing, electrical, HVAC).
- Explain how to identify potential issues early.

How to Spot Structural Damage:
- Show homeowners what signs of damage to look for in foundations, walls, and other structural elements.
- Explain the importance of timely repairs.

Gutter Cleaning and Maintenance:
- Demonstrate how to clean gutters and explain why it's important.
- Offer tips on how often to perform this task.

Energy-Efficient Home Improvements:
- Explain different types of energy-efficient home improvements (e.g., windows, insulation, HVAC systems).
- Discuss the benefits of energy efficiency, such as cost savings and environmental impact.

Choosing the Right Contractor:
- Provide tips on what to look for when hiring a contractor.
- Discuss questions homeowners should ask potential contractors.

Home Renovation Process:
- Walk through the steps involved in a typical home renovation.
- Explain what homeowners can expect during the process.

Seasonal Home Inspections:
- Offer advice on inspecting different parts of the home at different

times of the year.
- Explain what to look for in each season.

Common Home Problems and Solutions:
- Identify common issues (e.g., plumbing leaks, electrical problems) and their causes.
- Provide solutions or preventive measures homeowners can take.

DIY Home Repairs vs. Professional Repairs:
- Discuss minor repairs homeowners can safely do themselves.
- Explain when it's best to call a professional.

Impact of Weather on Homes:
- Explain how different weather conditions affect various parts of the home (e.g., siding, roofing, foundations).
- Offer tips on how to protect homes from extreme weather.

Importance of Proper Ventilation:
- Discuss how ventilation affects home health (e.g., mold prevention, energy efficiency).
- Explain how to ensure proper ventilation.

Upgrading to Sustainable Home Features:
- Provide information on sustainable home options (e.g., solar panels, rainwater harvesting systems).
- Discuss the benefits and considerations of sustainable features.

Home Improvement Myths and Facts:
- Debunk common myths about home improvements.
- Provide accurate information to educate homeowners.

How to File a Home Insurance Claim:
- Guide homeowners through the process of filing an insurance claim for various types of damage.
- Offer tips on working with insurance companies.

Budgeting for Home Repairs and Renovations:
- Provide advice on how to budget for major home repairs or renovations.
- Discuss financing options or savings tips.

Preventative Home Maintenance:
- Offer tips on regular maintenance to prevent bigger issues down the line (e.g., sealing cracks, checking for leaks).
- Discuss seasonal maintenance checklists.

Safety Tips for Home Projects:
- Provide safety guidelines for homeowners tackling DIY projects.
- Explain the importance of proper tools and protective equipment.

Understanding Building Codes and Permits:
- Explain the basics of building codes and why they matter.
- Discuss the process of obtaining necessary permits for home projects.
- Waterproofing and Moisture Control:
- Provide tips on how to protect basements, foundations, and crawl spaces from water damage.
- Explain the benefits of moisture control.

Enhancing Curb Appeal:
- Offer ideas for exterior improvements that enhance curb appeal (e.g., landscaping, painting, lighting).
- Discuss the impact of curb appeal on home value.

By creating these types of educational videos, contractors can address common homeowner concerns, showcase their expertise, and improve their search rankings on Google. Make sure to optimize your video titles, descriptions, and tags with relevant keywords to enhance SEO.

Business Attributes: Google Business Profile attributes play an important role in shaping the identity and visibility of your business. Adding business attributes to your Google Business Profile such as women-owned, veteran-owned, black-owned, and Latino-owned not only contribute to the diversity and inclusivity of your profile but also hold the potential to boost your business's visibility on Google.

Incorporating these attributes in your profile signals to Google that your business aligns with specific categories, making it eligible for inclusion in searches that prioritize diversity. Google recognizes the importance of diverse representation, and having these attributes can give your business a boost in relevant searches. It's a powerful way to highlight the unique aspects of your team.

Potential customers actively seek companies who resonate with their values, and Google's acknowledgment of these attributes enhances your chances of standing out. This recognition not only fosters a sense of community and connection but also contributes to creating a landscape that reflects the diversity of the population. So, embrace and proudly display these attributes on your Google Business Profile to make a positive impact on both your business and the broader community.

You can maximize the potential of your Google Business Profile by leveraging some of Google My Business features like posts and Q&A. Regularly update your profile with informative and engaging posts to keep it active and relevant. Share updates on new services or products. Utilize the Q&A section to address common queries and provide valuable information, demonstrating your commitment to safety and quality. By actively utilizing these features, you enhance your online presence, engage with your audience, and make it easier for potential homeowners to choose your business for their home improvement needs.

Beyond Google Business Profile - Online Directory Listings

Enhancing your business's visual appeal extends beyond Google Business. There are hundreds of other online business directory listings that are critical for local SEO including an array of platforms such as Apple Maps, Waze, Yelp, Bing, Facebook, Instagram, and even voice-activated systems like Siri and Alexa. Online directory listings for contractors serve as powerful sources of backlinks, significantly enhancing the overall Search Engine Optimization (SEO) standing. These listings act as digital checkpoints, each providing a valuable link back to the contractors website. Search engines, recognizing these backlinks as credible endorsements, assign higher authority to the website. As the website's authority increases, so does its visibility in search engine results.

For contractors navigating the competitive online landscape, backlinks from various directories, mapping systems, and social media platforms not only boost your digital presence but also significantly enhance your SEO. When optimized strategically, this network of listings creates a strong web of backlinks, ensuring your business stands out in relevant search queries and ultimately attracts more customers to your services.

Picture this scenario: A prospective customer is using their car's navigation system, relying on Apple Maps or Waze to find your location. Ensuring accurate information across these platforms is paramount. Unbeknownst to many, online directory listings play pivotal roles in various scenarios.

Imagine the frustration when a homeowner follows the directions provided by a navigation app in their car to visit your business, only to end up at an outdated address or wrong location. They get irritated and by the time they make it to you, they are in a negative mood.

People also rely on voice-activated systems like Siri or Alexa in their searches for contractors. A misstep in updating this information can also result in frustration.

What about all of the products you offer? Most of manufacturers have a "find-a-contractor" section on their websites. Are you listed as a contractor on their website? Reach out to your reps and make sure they have submitted you to their contractor finder directories!

Online listings are susceptible to user-generated suggestions and edits. From phone number changes to category modifications, contractors must be vigilant in accepting or rejecting these proposals. A proactive approach ensures the preservation of accurate information, thwarting potential disruptions caused by erroneous suggestions.

How to Develop Authority for your Map Listing via Directory Listings & Citation Development

Now that you have claimed your Google Business Profile Listing and optimized it to its fullest, you need to build authority.
Having a well-claimed and optimized local listing doesn't automatically rank you on page one. Google wants to list the most legitimate and qualified providers first. So, how do they figure out who gets the page one listings?

Well, there are a number of determining factors, but one of them is how widely the company is referenced on various online directory sites such as Yellow Pages, City Search, Yelp and others.

Citations are web references to your company name, address and phone number. You can add citations in a variety of ways. There are directory listings that you should claim manually and others that you can submit to via submission services like Universal Business Listing or Yext.com.

My personal preference is to claim listings manually, ensuring that I am in control and can make updates/edits as needed.

TOP Citation Sources to Claim Manually:
- Google Business Profile
- Bing Local
- Yahoo Local
- City Search
- FourSquare.com

- Yelp
- YP.com
- Merchant Circle
- Manta

List of the Top 50 Directory Listings and Citation Sources for Contractors

1) Google
Google is probably the most important and most talked about place to list your local business. Getting citations from many of the sites below (as well as ratings) can help boost your business' listing in Google.

2) Yelp
The most popular social networking, directory and review site. Aside from counting as a citation for your business in the eyes of major search engines, this site can deliver quite a bit of traffic on its own. However, business-owners using Yelp will need to learn to deal with the occasional nasty review.

3) Foursquare
A popular way to check-in to various locations using a smart phone. This can also provide a valuable citation for your local business.

4) Universal Business Listing
A local listing service – UBL.org (along with Localeze below) is one of the major players in the effort to only fill in your information once while getting listed on multiple yellow pages sites, directories and social networking/review sites. It saves time and effort but may be slower than going directly with the individual sites (see Localeze and InfoUSA below).

5) Yahoo Local
Yahoo's local directory tied to Yahoo Maps.

6) Local.com
Business listings, event listings, coupons and reviews.

7) CitySearch
One of the most authoritative local directories.

8) Bing Local
Bing's local business listing service integrated with maps of cities and towns.

9) Craigslist
Some recommend creating classifieds for your business on popular sites such as Craigslist. There's some disagreement over whether this is effective from an SEO point of view.

10) GetListed.org
Convenient way to identify where you are and are not listed in major directories. Provides referrals to Universal Business Listings and Localeze as well as consultants (if you need extra help).

11) DMOZ (Open Directory Project)
A free and authoritative index (in the eyes of Google) that is managed by volunteers.

If you can get your business listed, this helps with an authoritative backlink (but not necessarily a local citation). It can be difficult to get a new listing due to the limited resources and large volumes of submissions.

12) Superpages
One of the many Internet Yellow Pages directories (IYP). Includes business listings, people search, reviews and local deals.

13) Localeze
A multiple local listing service.

14) InfoUSA
A multiple local listings service.

15) Your local Chamber of Commerce

Joining your local chamber of commerce can often get you a business listing (and a citation for local SEO purposes)

16) InsiderPages
Local directory and rating site.

17) Merchant Circle
Local directory and rating site.

18) Best of the Web
A popular directory with free and paid listing options – specifically for local, they have a Best of the Web Local directory.

19) Yellowpages.com
Internet yellow pages (also YP.com).

20) Judys Book
Social search and online yellow pages

21) Business.com
Business.com provides business information but also has a business directory.

22) Better Business Bureau
Your local Better Business Bureaus will usually charge for membership and provide a link to your business.

23) DexKnows
Business and people directory.

24) Your local newspaper's website
Getting an article, business listing or classified ad optimized with your local information and a link can provide a citation for your business.

25) Yellowbook.com
Internet yellow pages.

26) HotFrog
A business directory with free and fairly inexpensive paid listing options.

27) Crunchbase
A listing of technology companies that is user generated.

28) Angi's List
Service provider directory.

29) Jigsaw
Businesspeople and company directory.

30) iBegin
US and Canadian business directory.

31) Wikimapia
Wiki-based directory of places including schools, businesses, and more – laid out on maps.

32) CitySquares
Local business directory with ratings.

33) InfoSpace
Business and people listings.

34) MagicYellow
A straightforward Internet yellow pages directory.

35) Whitepages.com
People and business listings.

36) Manta
Company profiles.

37) EZLocal
Local business listings and ratings.

38) BrownBook
Local business listings and ratings.

39) CityVoter
Vote for favorite businesses.

40) ShopCity
Local business listings.

41) YellowBot
Local listings and ratings.

42) GetFave
Business directory, including featured listings (with additional content such as videos and pictures).

43) BizJournals
Business journal that includes business directories for certain US cities.

44) Tjoos
Online store listings and coupons.

45) JoeAnt
Website directory.

46) Zidster
Products, services or business listings.

47) TrueLocal
Business directory – seems to have sparse listings.

48) GoMyLocal
Yellow pages/local directory.

49) City Slick
Free business directory.

50) Home Advisor
Directory of service companies (includes a "seal of approval").
By securing these high-quality citations you will boost your authority and highly improve your probability of ranking in the Google Map Listings. The next critical step is to get online reviews!

As a home contractor, maintaining a consistent online presence is crucial. Ensure your business name, categories, and descriptions are uniform across all platforms. This consistency helps improve search engine rankings and eliminates confusion for potential customers looking for specific home services.

Contractors starting their digital journey need to look beyond just Google. Navigating various online directories, including mapping systems, voice-activated platforms, and social media directories, is crucial. As the manager of your online presence, maintain consistency, respond promptly to reviews, and actively manage your digital footprint to stand out in the competitive home services industry.

BONUS! Watch our Webinar on
"The Ultimate SEO Playbook For Home Services Contractors"

https://nailitmarketing.agency/seo-webinar

Chapter 6
Your Online Reputation & Why It Matters

When homeowners are searching for a reliable contractor, they often conduct thorough research to ensure they're making the right choice. Online reviews are a key component of this decision-making process. It's essential for contractors—whether in roofing, painting, plumbing, handyman services, electrical work, or HVAC—to actively manage their online reputation, encourage positive reviews, and address any concerns to meet the expectations of informed homeowners.

Importance of Google and Yelp Reviews
While various review platforms exist, the majority of customers turn to Google when evaluating and selecting a contractor. It's crucial for contractors to prioritize soliciting reviews on their Google Business Profile due to its widespread usage and significant impact on local search visibility. Additionally, Yelp serves as a valuable secondary option, catering to those who may not have a Gmail email address, which is required for leaving Google reviews. By strategically focusing efforts on these prominent platforms, contractors can maximize their online presence and effectively engage with potential customers.

Impact on SEO and Business Growth

Google reviews also contribute significantly to the search engine optimization (SEO) of a contractor's online presence. Positive reviews signal credibility and relevance to search engines, improving the chances of ranking higher in search results. This visibility is crucial for attracting new customers, especially in the competitive home services industry.

For homeowners navigating the complex landscape of choosing a contractor, trust is paramount. Positive Google reviews act as real-life testimonials, offering reassurance to potential customers. They highlight the quality of work, professionalism, and overall customer experience, making it easier for homeowners to make informed decisions about who they invite into their homes.

Complementing Marketing Efforts

Investing in marketing efforts without managing online reputation can create a bottleneck in converting potential customers. A robust online presence, fueled by positive Google reviews, not only complements marketing strategies but also serves as a foundational element for customer conversion.

Getting Reviews

5 Free Strategies to Generate More Google Reviews:
1. QR Codes: Create a QR code that links to your Google Business Profile review URL. Place these codes on business cards, invoices, and hand them out after your jobs. This allows customers to easily leave reviews by scanning the code. This provides a convenient and immediate way for satisfied customers to share their experiences.
2. Staff Engagement: Empower your phone staff and crew to ask customers about their experience during the job's completion. If positive, encourage them to scan the QR code for a Google review, creating a seamless process.
3. Social Media Testimonials: Leverage your social media platforms to showcase customer testimonials. Once a week, post a customer testimonial on Facebook, Instagram, and LinkedIn, and include your Google review link in posts, encouraging followers to share their positive experiences online.

4. Follow-up Emails and SMS Campaigns: Implement automated email and SMS campaigns post-service, seeking customer feedback. For those expressing satisfaction, provide a direct link to leave a Google review.
5. Website and Invoices: Include a link to your Google Business Profile in your email signature, on your website, and on printed invoices. This constant presence serves as a reminder for customers to leave a review.

Simple Steps to Use When Asking for Reviews:
1. Ask for a Favor: Ask the customer if they will do you a favor and write a review.
2. Keep It Short: Tell them it will take less than 5 minutes.
3. Explain the Benefit: Explain how your business and others in the community would benefit from their review.
4. Make It Easy: Tell them the easiest way to write a review (use their phone, or click a link in an email you will send).
5. Show Gratitude: Thank them and let them know you look forward to reading their comments.

Using Email to Get More Reviews
We have found that the best time to ask for that email address is at the point of booking the service. If you wait until after the service is rendered your technicians on-site will say "OK, thanks for the money, by the way give me your email address". They are going to say, "Why do you need my email address?" "Oh, because I want to ask you for a review or…" There is a lot of resistance to it at that point in the process.

However, if you move into the front where somebody calls in and says, "Hey I need to schedule a service, my house is flooded." You can respond, "We can get somebody out there right away. Let me gather your information."

This is the perfect time to get the email address. Typically, you get their name, address, and the phone number. Well, you can just add one more step at that point and request an email address as well. You can tell them that it is so you can send a confirmation.

That's how you start to develop a database of emails. We are going to talk about email marketing later in the book as part of your online marketing plan, but for this purpose, you need an email address so that you can send a message after service thanking them for their business and asking them to write you a review.

The number of reviews that you have from actual customers is going to increase exponentially if you repeat this process regularly. This is how you are going to start to really dominate the Google Map, because reviews and citations work in harmony for ranking.

To get a nice bump in the number of reviews, develop an email list of friends, family, and customers who have been with you for quite some time. People you know, like, and trust, who would be willing to act on your behalf.

Put together that email list in an Excel sheet. It might be ten contacts, or it might be 700 contacts. Include the names and email addresses of these people. Then, use a tool like Constant Contact, MailChimp, or another email marketing tool to send an email blast with the following message:

Subject: Your Feedback Matters – Share Your Experience with [Contractor's Name]

Dear [Customer's Name],

I hope this email finds you well. At [Your Company], we are committed to providing exceptional service and continuously strive to enhance the customer experience. We value your opinion and would greatly appreciate it if you could take a few moments to share your experience with us. Your feedback not only helps us maintain the high standard of service we aim for but also assists other homeowners in choosing the right contractor for their needs. We believe in the power of shared experiences, and your review can make a significant impact.

To leave a review, simply click on the following link: [Insert Google Re-

view Link]

Thank you for being a part of the [Your Company] community. Your insights are instrumental in helping us continually enhance our services.

Best regards,
[Your Name]
[Your Title/Role]
[Your Company]
[Contact Information]

Responding to Reviews

When someone leaves you a review on Google, you can see it and respond. Timely review monitoring is crucial. Responding to reviews, especially negative ones, within 24-48 hours demonstrates a commitment to customer satisfaction.

There are some essential things to remember when responding to reviews:
- Keep it professional. Don't air dirty laundry in your review response!
- The response should not discuss the specifics of the job but should be generic.

Example Responses to Positive Reviews:
"Thank you for sharing your review! We strive to provide the best possible service to every customer, and always enjoy reading about a good experience."

"Wow – thanks for your kind remarks! We thrive on this type of feedback, so we'll be sure to pass this review off to the team. Thanks again!"
"Thank you for this feedback. Our company has an amazing group of professionals, and we all take great pride in our work."

"Thank you for taking the time to share this review! We take great pride in providing exceptional service to all of our customers and appreciate your kind words."

Example Responses to Negative Reviews:
"Our policy is to schedule plenty of time between jobs to avoid delays. We strive to deliver the best service possible to all our customers, but we occasionally fall behind schedule. We value your feedback and want to thank you for taking the time to share it. You can call our office and ask for our Manager [NAME] if you have any further comments or suggestions."

"Thank you for taking the time to provide feedback. We strive to make each customer's experience exceptional, and it pains us to hear if we fall short of a customer's expectations. Please call our office at (XXX) XXX-XXXX to discuss this matter further."

"Thank you for bringing this to our attention. We take all feedback seriously. We encourage you to contact us directly to discuss your concerns further. We value our customers and their feedback, and we hope to have the opportunity to address any issues and improve your experience with our services."

Google reviews are not just testimonials but pivotal elements in a comprehensive digital marketing strategy. For homeowners seeking trustworthy contractors, positive reviews instill confidence, making your business stand out and reinforcing the reliability that every customer seeks.
In the next chapter, we're diving into social media—the heartbeat of your online engagement. Let's go!

Chapter 7
Overview of Paid Online Advertising Opportunities

If we revisit the Online Marketing Plan referenced in chapter one of this book, you will recall that the foundation of your Internet marketing plan should be focused on the organic, non-paid marketing efforts (Website, SEO, Google Maps, Social Media Marketing, Video Marketing, etc.)

Once you have a strong foundation, you should have the financial resources to invest in other paid online marketing initiatives.

In this next chapter, I want to quickly recap the paid online marketing options you should consider:

- Pay-Per-Click Marketing on Google Ads and Microsoft Search (Bing)
- Google Local Service Ads
- Paid online directory listings on sites like MerchantLocal, Yelp.com, YP.com, BBB
- Pay-Per-Lead and Lead Aggregators like Angi, Thumbtack, Networx

Now, let's talk about the most powerful of these strategies – Pay-Per-Click Marketing.

Chapter 8

Pay-Per-Click Marketing (Google Ads and Bing Search) Contractors for Home Service

In this chapter, we will explore Pay-Per-Click (PPC) marketing, its benefits, and how you can effectively use it to drive profitable business for your home services company, whether you specialize in roofing, painting, plumbing, electrical work, or handyman services.

Why PPC Should Be Part of Your Overall Marketing Strategy
- Start showing up quickly
- Show up as often as possible where your customers are looking
- Show up for non-geo-modified terms that are related to your service offering.

First, PPC gets things happening quickly, unlike an SEO program, setting up your website, building links and having the right on-page optimization. That process takes a little bit of time to materialize. What you do today and tomorrow, will start to pay dividends in three to four months.

With PPC advertising, you set up your campaign and will start to see your ads serve in just a few days. It can drive good traffic, especially during the times when you need to make sure you're visible. We looked at the differences between the paid listings, the organic listings and the map listings. You want to show up as often as possible when someone's looking for your services. Having a pay per click ad that shows up somewhere in the top, on the map, and in the organic section is important.

Now you've got the opportunity to show up in multiple places and significantly improve the chances of getting your ad clicked on, as opposed to your competition. A pay-per-click campaign gives you that additional placeholder on the search engines on page one.

It also gives you the opportunity to show up for words that you're not going to show up for in your organic SEO efforts. This is what I like to call non geo-modified keywords.

SEO and our whole organic strategy give us the ability to show up in search engines when someone types in your city service, for e.g. your city plumber, your city electrician, your city handyman, etc. All of those include some kind of geo modifier (your city). They're going to put their city or their sub-city in that search for you to rank.

With a PPC campaign, you can show up for the non-geo-modified terms (Example: interior painting, exterior painting, caulking, priming, etc.), and put in the settings that you only want to show up for people within a 25-mile radius of your office.

If you're in Miami and somebody searches within that area for "painting contractor" or "interior painting," you can set it so that it only shows your ad for the people that are searching within that area. And Google can manage that through IP addresses by isolating where the search took place.

Google can also isolate who ran that search, where they ran that search from, and then place the ads based on the advertisers that are set up for that area.

You only pay on a per click basis, but you're able to show up for those keywords in those major markets. Another reason that you want to consider running a pay per click campaign is because you can run mobile PPC campaigns.

With mobile PPC campaigns, when somebody is searching for your services from a mobile device, it's typically because they need immediate service. They're not as apt to browse multiple pages or listings. Now, if somebody runs a search on their mobile device, and you have a pay-per-click campaign set up, that search will be PPC enabled.

They can simply hit your ad and automatically be calling your company, rather than browsing to your website and researching.

On a pay-per-click campaign through mobile, you're actually paying per call as opposed to paying per lead. It's very powerful, and these are the reasons you want to have pay-per-click as part of your overall Internet marketing plan.

Understanding PPC Networks

GOOGLE VS. BING: WHICH ONE ARE YOUR CUSTOMERS USING?

Google	USER TRAITS	bing
Generally white collar		Generally blue collar
More techy		Less techy
Younger than 35		Older than 35
University/college-educated		17% of Canadian searches

	PAY-PER-CLICK ADVERTISING	
More volume of searches!		Less volume
More competition		Mainly used by Americans
More worldwide reach		Less competition, easier to stand out
More expensive (avg. $1.83/click)		Less expensive (avg. $1.07/click)

ABORG

There are two major PPC networks:
- Google Ads: Covers Google and its partner sites like AOL, AT&T, USA Today, and Ask.com.
- Bing Ads: Includes Bing, Yahoo!, and other Microsoft Search Network partners.

More than 80 percent of all searches happen on Google.com. So, if you had to choose, you would obviously you want to use Google. However, you do get an additional 20 percent by tapping into Bing and Yahoo!

There are different networks but those two make up the majority of the search market. Running a pay-per-click campaign on both Google AdWords and Microsoft Bing search will allow you to show up in the majority of the search engines that somebody might be using.

How Google Ads Work

Google Ads operate on an auction system where you bid on keywords. Your ad position is determined by your bid amount and the quality score, which is influenced by:

- Click-Through Rate (CTR): The percentage of people who click on your ad.
- Relevance: How relevant your ad text is to the keywords being searched.

- Landing Page Quality: The relevance and quality of the page your ad directs users to.

Let's review how Google AdWords works.
In the simplest sense, you're paying on a per click basis and you can choose your keywords (Example: roofer, your city electrician, your city emergency plumber). As you pick those words, you bid, and you pay on a per click basis.

So, let's just say you're bidding on the keywords "San Antonio Electrician," and there are a lot of other electricians in that city that want to rank for that keyword.

If you say that you'll pay $2.00/click and your competitor says that they'll pay $5.00/click, they're going to be at the top. Assuming nobody else has placed a higher bid, $2.00 is going to be ranked second and $1.20 is going to follow.

I am about to explain why that isn't 100% of the reality. The fact is that you pay on per click basis and you are bidding against the competitors to determine how you're going to rank on your keyword.

It's an auction, just like eBay. People are bidding and whoever can offer the most money is going to have the strong position. With that foundational understanding, we can now explain why most pay-per-click campaigns fail.

What tends to happen is a lot of pay-per-click campaigns are built on the notion that the highest bid wins. So, advertisers pick their keywords, throw up the highest bid per click and hope that everything turns out the way they want it.

Common PPC Mistakes
- Setup only ONE ad group for all services
- Don't use specific text ads and landing pages for groups of keywords
- No strong call to action or OFFER on the landing page

You might be thinking, you just told me that PPC is a great way to get noticed, and now you're saying that most campaigns fail! I'm going to explain what people do wrong and then show you what to do right so that your campaign is successful.

Typically, businesses setup only one ad group for all services, whether it's plumber, drain cleaning, emergency plumber, residential plumber, etc. instead of different ad groups for each type of service.

Also, there's no specific text ads and no landing pages for those ad groups and groups of keywords.

What you wind up with is the same landing page and the same text ad, whether your customer typed in "plumber, water heater repair, emergency plumber, drain cleaning, etc." in the search engine.

Whatever was typed into the search engine was likely very specific, and should match up to a very specific page, but that doesn't happen. It all goes to the home page. With this strategy, not only is your campaign going to convert poorly, but your cost per click is going to be higher. I will explain why later in this chapter.

The other reason why most pay-per-click campaigns fail is because there isn't a strong call-to-action on the landing page. So, you were just charged $5.00 or $9.00 to get a potential customer to your website and the page isn't even compelling because it does not have a strong call-to-action. It doesn't tell the consumer what to do next.

If you factor these common reasons that pay-per-click campaigns tend to fail, you can better prepare yourself and set yourself up for success in the way that you execute your pay per click marketing.

Setting Up a Successful PPC Campaign
1. Ad Groups Based on Services: Create specific ad groups for each service you offer (e.g., roof repair, plumbing services, electrical work).
2. Relevant Text Ads: Write text ads that are relevant to the keywords and ad groups.
3. Specific Landing Pages: Drive traffic to landing pages that match the keywords and ad group, with compelling content and a strong call to action.

Best Practices for Google Ads Setup
1. Use Ad Extensions: Add your address, phone number, and links to important pages to make your ad more informative.
2. Multiple Text Ads: Create multiple text ads for each ad group to split test and find the most effective one.
3. Monitor Average Position: Aim to maintain a top-four position in search results for optimal visibility.
4. Exact Match Keywords: Use exact match keywords to ensure your ads appear for relevant searches.
5. Negative Keywords: Exclude irrelevant searches by using negative keywords.

Phone Searches versus Computer Searches
More and more people are accessing the Internet via smart devices: their iPhone, Android, and tablets. The searcher is typically in a different mindframe when they are searching from a phone rather than from the computer.

When you're searching from a phone, you often just want to get the information right away, and/or want your problem solved as soon as possible. You can set up a campaign to have click-to-call built into your mobile campaign.

Set up a mobile-specific campaign and choose "Mobile Devices Only." Then you can pick your geolocation. That would be your 30-mile range or 20-mile radius. You then click a button to turn on the click-to-call function.

That's how you wind up with a pay-per-click campaign that has you in the top positions if you bid correctly, with the options for them to do a click-to-call.

Why Hiring a Google Ads Specialist is Beneficial

Google Ads can be complex and time-consuming to manage effectively. Here are some reasons why hiring a Google Ads specialist, like those at Nail It Marketing Pros, can help you get the most out of your campaigns:

1. Expertise and Experience: Google Ads specialists have the knowledge and experience to set up and manage campaigns efficiently, ensuring you get the best results.
2. Optimization: Specialists continuously monitor and optimize your campaigns, making adjustments to improve performance and reduce costs.
3. Advanced Strategies: They can implement advanced strategies like ad scheduling, geotargeting, and remarketing that may be difficult to manage on your own.
4. Time Savings: Managing Google Ads campaigns can be time-consuming. Hiring a specialist allows you to focus on running your business while they handle the marketing.
5. Better ROI: With professional management, you are more likely to see a better return on investment, as campaigns are optimized for performance and cost-effectiveness.

Nail It Marketing Pros offers comprehensive Google Ads management services for home service contractors. Our team of specialists can help you set up and run effective PPC campaigns, ensuring you get the best results for your investment.

Just to recap, you want to:
- Set up your ad groups correctly.
- Make sure that you pick keywords that group them together
- You write text ads that speak directly to that group of keywords, and
- Ensure your landing page (where you are sending those specific searches) speaks to the text ads and the group of keywords.
- You also want to be sure that you have some type of strong call-to-action that prompts your consumer into calling you as opposed to pressing the "Back" button and looking at four or five other competitors.

As the relevancy of your ad groups campaign and your keywords improve, your cost-per-click will decline and your conversion will improve.

You can spend less and still get better positioning and more traffic to your website. By following the strategies outlined in this chapter, you can maximize the profitability of your PPC campaigns, ensuring they contribute effectively to your overall marketing efforts.

Chapter 9

Paid Online Directories - Which Ones Should You Consider?

In this chapter, we will explore paid online directory listings. We've already discussed the overall Internet marketing strategy, starting with the foundation of a properly optimized website. This includes having the right pages, conversion elements, off-page optimization for building inbound links, building domain authority, and implementing a review acquisition strategy to rank in organic, non-pay-per-click listings for your most important keywords.

We will also explore social media and email marketing as ways to connect with your customers on a deeper level and generate more repeat and referral business. Once you have these non-paid elements of your Internet marketing strategy in place, you can start looking at paid online marketing programs.

We've covered pay-per-click marketing and how to set up effective PPC campaigns on Google Ads or Microsoft Bing to appear in paid listings. Now, let's delve into other paid marketing components, such as online directory listings that you can pay for to get premium placements.

There are hundreds of online directories, from Yelp.com and Foursquare to City Search and BBB, as well as various smaller secondary directories. We'll focus on the most prominent and visited directories that can help you gain exposure where your customers are looking the most.

Paid Online Directory Listings You Should Consider

Criteria: Active business profile, positive reviews, consistent engagement.

Application Process: Create and verify your business profile on Yelp. Encourage satisfied customers to leave positive reviews. Consider paying for premium ad placement to increase visibility.

Yelp is one of the best review sites for local businesses. If you want customers to find your business online, you need to be on Yelp. Yelp allows you to send public or private messages (including deals) to customers and review business trends using the Yelp reporting tool. If you have many reviews on Yelp, paying for a premium ad can help enhance your service visibility.

Criteria: Business profile, local presence, consistent engagement.

Application Process: Create and verify your business profile on YP.com. Avoid being roped into their print Yellow Page ads, which can be costly.

Focus on online listings and avoid letting them manage your pay-per-click advertising.

The online yellow pages vary by area. In some markets, it's YP.com; in others, it might be DexKnows.com, Version Yellow Pages, or YellowBook.com. Be careful when getting started to avoid high costs associated with print ads and poorly managed PPC campaigns.

Criteria: Business profile, active engagement, relevance to local searches. Application Process: Create and verify your business profile on City Search. Optimize your listing with detailed information and high-quality images.

City Search specializes in listings for various businesses, including restaurants, bars, spas, hotels, and other service providers across the U.S. It optimizes these listings via a partner network that includes Expedia and MerchantCircle.

Criteria: Ethical business practices, positive customer feedback, adherence to BBB standards.

Application Process: Apply for BBB accreditation by completing an online application and meeting their standards for trust. Display the BBB logo and maintain good standing.

BBB is a major sign of credibility. Posting the BBB logo and being able to say that you're A+ accredited adds to your business's reputation. It might not generate a ton of leads, but it's a great credibility symbol and a good reference point for potential customers.

Criteria: Active business profile, positive customer engagement, consistent updates.

Application Process: Create and verify your business profile on Foursquare. Encourage customers to check in and leave reviews.

Foursquare provides listings for all kinds of local businesses. It has a significant user base, with 93 percent of local storefronts and over 50 million site visitors.

Criteria: Business profile, engagement with local consumers, positive reviews.

Application Process: Create and verify your business profile on MerchantCircle. Engage with the platform and encourage customers to leave reviews.

MerchantCircle allows people to find the best local merchants. The site includes listings for a wide range of business owners and is visited by over 100 million consumers annually.

Pay-Per-Lead and Lead Services - How to Properly Manage Pay-Per-Lead Services for Maximum Return and Long-term Gains

Now let's talk about pay-per-lead services. With these services, you can pay per lead or on a monthly basis to gain access to all the leads that come into your market. If you need additional leads or have an inside sales team that can proactively follow up, these are good options:

- Angi
- Home Advisor
- Thumbtack
- Service Direct
- Nextdoor
- Porch
- Handy

How Do Pay-Per-Lead Services Work?
The nice thing about this type of service is that you only pay when you get a qualified lead. With others, you just have a budget. For example, you set $500.00/month to get all of the leads that come in from that area. Most of these pay-per-lead service providers have combined experience in working with a wide range of industries including automotive, law, healthcare, and other sectors.

If you've followed the plan outlined in this book, you should have your organic keywords ranking well in the search engines and map listings, proactive social media and email marketing, and a well-structured pay-per-click marketing campaign. If you want to boost lead flow, these services can help start channeling new customers looking for your services. However, you must be diligent and quick with your follow-up.

You will hear a lot of horror stories about how poorly these lead services work and how they can waste money. If you've built your Internet marketing strategy on pay-per-lead services alone, you're destined to fail. You can't build a sustainable business around just this one strategy. But, as an addon to a strong Internet marketing program, they can be relatively effective. Remember, these leads aren't coming directly to you; they are often sent anonymously. They might be price-conscious shoppers looking for the lowest price. Keep that in mind.

Fast Follow Up Is Critical

If you don't have the time and energy to chase leads, consider passing on pay-per-lead services altogether. These leads go out to you and a number of other companies in your area, so you have to be aggressive. Be the first person to get customers on the phone and be professional with a compelling offer that makes them choose you over the competition.

Create a follow-up system to ensure you have a fallback plan for leads you can't reach right away. Leads can come in various formats: email, downloadable Excel lists, or text message alerts. Assign a marketing manager or a specific team member to follow up on leads, ensuring no lead falls through the cracks. Have a predefined script on how calls should be handled. Be professional, courteous, and quick.

Many leads will go to the first person that gets them on the phone, so being aggressive is essential. Don't just call once. Have a process to reach out 3 to 5 times over 24 hours because they are in the window to buy. If you don't get them on the phone, take note of their name and email address to remain top-of-mind.

Stay in Touch

You've got their name and email address, so market to these leads via email on at least a monthly basis. Build an email database of customers and prospects and send out updates regularly. Include special offers to remain top-of-mind and build your customer base.

As you look at paid online advertising and pay-per-lead services, be cautious. Don't overspend. Ensure you have tracking in place to measure return on investment. If you choose to use pay-per-lead services, have a proactive and diligent process that touches these people multiple times via phone and email.

Chapter 10
Social Media Mastery for Contractors

In the dynamic landscape of marketing for home services contractors, social media has emerged as a powerful tool. It's not merely a platform; it's a dynamic space where contractors can amplify their influence, foster customer relationships, and curate a distinctive online presence. As we delve deeper into the realms of social media marketing, remember that authenticity, engagement, and education form the cornerstone of your digital success.

The Benefits of a Dedicated Business Page

A Window to Professional Excellence
Your social media business pages serve as a digital canvas where you can showcase the essence of your business and the amazing results you get for your customers. Unlike personal profiles, a business page empowers you to share educational content, impactful videos, before and after photos, tips, and essential information about your services.

Unlock the "Recommendation" Advantage
One of the notable features of social media business pages is the invaluable "recommendation" feature. This element amplifies the voice of sat-

isfied customers, providing genuine endorsements that resonate with your audience.

Behind-the-Scenes Connection

Social media serves as the backstage pass for customers to glimpse the inner workings of your business. It's a platform to convey the personality behind the brand, the spectrum of services offered, and the specialized expertise that defines your business.

Consistency with Branding and Website

Your social media business pages should seamlessly align with your branding and website. Ensure comprehensive listings of the services you provide, accompanied by regular content updates. Consistency fosters engagement, building a loyal following over time.

Educational, Not Salesy

Avoid the pitfall of transforming your social media into a sales pitch. Instead, share content that educates, resonates, and provides a personal touch. Remember, social media is a narrative, not a sales brochure.

Platform-Specific Strategies

Facebook: Connecting with the Community

Why Facebook Matters: Homeowners dominate the usage of Facebook, actively engaging on this platform. Establishing a Facebook business page allows you to share educational content, tips, and behind-the-scenes glimpses of your work and team.

Benefits:

- Educational Content: Share articles, videos, and infographics to educate your audience about roofing, painting, plumbing, and more.
- Recommendation Feature: Leverage the "recommendation" feature to build trust, as positive reviews can influence potential customers.
- Brand Visibility: Provide a window into your business, showcasing

your brand, services, and expertise.

The Power of Local Facebook Groups:
Facebook groups are community powerhouses, providing unique opportunities for contractors to connect with local homeowners and position themselves as trusted members of the community. Here's how to leverage these groups effectively:

1. Finding Your Niche: Identify the specific niche or demographic you want to target, such as home improvement or local community groups.
2. Joining Local Groups: Use Facebook's search feature to find active local groups with a significant number of members.
3. Observe, Engage, Connect: Understand the dynamics of the groups, engage authentically, and offer valuable home improvement tips. Be helpful - you will stand out!
4. Promoting Your Services: Share valuable information and occasionally highlight your services or promotions.
5. Collaborating with Group Administrators: Partner with group admins to ensure your engagement aligns with group guidelines.

Instagram: Visual Storytelling for Home Services
With its emphasis on visual content, Instagram is ideal for showcasing the quality of your work and the personality behind your business. Understanding the differences between posts, reels, and stories is crucial for creating a well-rounded and effective Instagram strategy:

1. Instagram Post:
- Format: Static images or videos (up to 60 seconds).
- Purpose: Showcase your services, share educational content, highlight customer testimonials, or provide updates.
- Tips: Use high-quality visuals, captivating captions, relevant hashtags, and include a call-to-action (CTA).

2. Instagram Reel:
- Format: Short-form videos (up to 60 seconds).
- Purpose: Create fun and engaging content, educational snippets, or behind-the-scenes looks.

- Tips: Leverage trends, keep it concise, and add music or voiceovers.

3. Instagram Story:
- Format: Vertical images or videos (up to 15 seconds per segment).
- Purpose: Share real-time updates, event promotions, or day-in-the-life content.
- Tips: Use features like polls, quizzes, and questions to encourage interaction.

Tips for Contractors Using Instagram:

- Visual Consistency: Maintain a consistent visual style and color palette.
- Educational Content: Share bite-sized educational content related to your services.
- customer Stories and Testimonials: Feature customer success stories to build trust.
- Interactive Content: Use interactive features to engage with your audience.
- Timely and Relevant Content: Stay updated with current trends and share timely information.
- Seasonal Promotions: Promote special offers, or seasonal services.
- Community Engagement: Engage with your community by responding to comments and participating in relevant conversations.
- Consistent Posting Schedule: Establish a consistent posting schedule to keep your audience engaged.

YouTube: Education through Video Content

Creating a YouTube channel for your contracting business can be a powerful strategy to enhance online presence, educate customers, and improve Google search ranking. Here's why and how contractors can benefit from having a YouTube channel:

- Visual Education: Create engaging content to educate customers about various home services topics.
- customer Engagement: Video content helps build a stronger connection with customers, fostering trust and credibility.

- Improved Google Search Ranking: Optimized videos positively impact your overall online visibility.
- Reach a Wider Audience: Tailored content can help you reach a wider demographic and attract new customers.
- Educational Series and Webinars: Host educational series and webinars on home improvement topics.
- Testimonials and Success Stories: Share customer testimonials and success stories to build trust.
- Collaborate with Influencers: Collaborate with industry influencers to expand your reach.
- YouTube Analytics Insights: Use analytics tools to refine your content strategy.
- Mobile Accessibility: Cater to on-the-go users with easily accessible videos.

LinkedIn: Professional Networking and Expertise Showcase
LinkedIn is a powerful platform for contractors to build a professional network, connect with suppliers, reach potential customers, and engage with industry professionals. Here are some best practices for utilizing LinkedIn effectively:

- Optimize Your Profile: Ensure your profile is complete and professional.
- Highlight Expertise: Clearly articulate your specialization in your profile summary.
- Connect with Industry Professionals: Actively connect with other professionals in your industry.
- Engage in LinkedIn Groups: Join and participate in LinkedIn groups related to home services.
- Share Educational Content: Share articles, research, and educational content related to your services.
- Showcase customer Success Stories: Highlight customer success stories to build trust.
- Collaborate with Suppliers: Connect with suppliers and explore potential collaborations.
- Publish Articles and Updates: Share your expertise by publishing arti-

cles or regular updates.
- Use LinkedIn Ads Strategically: Consider using targeted LinkedIn ads to reach specific demographics.

TikTok: Capturing Attention with Creativity
TikTok has become a powerful platform for content creators, including contractors, to engage with a wide audience. Here's how contractors can effectively use TikTok:

- Educational Content: Share short, informative videos on home services topics.
- Myth-Busting: Address common misconceptions or debunk myths.
- Personalized Insights: Share behind-the-scenes glimpses of your work.
- Challenges and Trends: Participate in TikTok challenges and trends.
- customer Testimonials: Share customer success stories (with consent).
- Q&A Sessions: Host question-and-answer sessions to engage with your audience.
- Leveraging Humor: Incorporate humor into your content while maintaining accuracy and sensitivity.
- Promotion of Services and Events: Promote events or new services.

Finding Your Followers

Building Initial Engagement
To leverage social media effectively, you need to gain an initial following. Here's a step-by-step process:

1. Leverage Email: Export the names and email addresses of your customers, including current and past customers, friends, business partners, and other contacts.
2. Email Campaign: Send a personalized email inviting them to follow your social media profiles. Offer an incentive, such as a discount or coupon, to encourage engagement.
3. Automated Follow-Up: Include automated follow-up emails reminding customers to engage with your social media profiles.

Consistent Posting

Post to your social media profiles regularly. If daily posts are too much, aim for at least once or twice a week. Ensure your posts are informative and not overly promotional. Here are some content ideas:

- Tips and Advice: Share expert tips related to your services.
- Project Photos: Post before-and-after photos of your projects.
- Behind-the-Scenes: Share glimpses of your daily operations.
- Customer Testimonials: Highlight positive feedback from customers.
- Team member of the week: Recognize your team members

Engaging with Your Audience

Engagement is key to social media success. Actively respond to comments, messages, and reviews. Engage in conversations and listen to your audience. Here are some engagement tips:

- Respond Promptly: Quickly reply to comments and messages.
- Acknowledge Feedback: Thank customers for positive feedback and address any concerns they may have.
- Personal Touch: Add a personal touch to your responses to build rapport.

Consistency and Branding

Maintain consistency across all your social media platforms. Ensure that your branding, color scheme, and messaging are uniform and aligned with your overall business identity. This creates a cohesive online presence that strengthens your brand recognition.

25 Social Media Story or Reel Ideas for Home Services Contractors:

1. Behind the Scenes: Take your audience behind the scenes of your daily operations, showcasing your team, tools, and workspaces.
2. Customer Success Stories: Share brief testimonials or success stories from satisfied customers (with permission) to build trust and show the positive impact of your services.
3. Day in the Life: Document a day in the life of a contractor to give fol-

lowers a glimpse into your daily routine and work process.
4. Home Maintenance Myth Busting: Debunk common myths or misconceptions related to home maintenance and improvement.
5. Industry News Updates: Share updates on the latest trends, innovations, or regulations in the home services industry.
6. DIY Tips: Share quick and easy do-it-yourself tips for homeowners to handle minor repairs and maintenance tasks.
7. Community Involvement: Highlight any local events, charity work, or community projects you're involved in.
8. Seasonal Maintenance Tips: Share tips and advice for maintaining homes during different seasons, such as winterizing pipes or summer AC maintenance.
9. Contractor's Recommended Tools: Share recommendations for essential tools and equipment that homeowners should have for basic home maintenance.
10. Flashback Friday: Share throwback videos or images from significant projects or milestones in your career.
11. Tool Talk Tuesday: Use Tuesdays to showcase and explain the tools of your trade, how they work, and why they are essential.
12. Project Walkthroughs: Walk through ongoing or completed projects, explaining the work done and the challenges faced.
13. Safety Tips: Share important safety tips for homeowners when dealing with home repairs and maintenance.
14. customer Q&A: Answer frequently asked questions from customers about your services, processes, and industry standards.
15. Before and After: Show before-and-after transformations of your projects to highlight your work quality and impact.
16. Eco-Friendly Home Tips: Share advice on making homes more energy-efficient and environmentally friendly.
17. Emergency Repair Tips: Provide tips on how homeowners can handle common home emergencies until professional help arrives.
18. Material Choices Explained: Explain the different materials used in your projects, their benefits, and why you choose them.
19. Home Improvement FAQs: Address frequently asked questions about home improvement, renovation, and repair projects.
20. Contractor's Checklist: Share a checklist for homeowners to follow

for regular home maintenance.
21. Tool Maintenance Tips: Provide tips on how to maintain and care for tools and equipment properly.
22. Meet the Team: Introduce the different members of your team, highlighting their roles and expertise.
23. Seasonal Project Ideas: Suggest home improvement projects that are ideal for different seasons.
24. Customer Reviews: Highlight positive reviews from customers to build credibility and trust.
25. Project Planning Tips: Share tips on how homeowners can effectively plan and prepare for home improvement projects.

Script for 60-Second Instagram or Facebook Videos
Hi, this is [Your Name] from [Your Company], and today I wanted to share with you 3 tips for maintaining your home this season.

Tip #1: [Tip #1]
Tip #2: [Tip #2]
Tip #3: [Tip #3]

If you'd like to learn more about home maintenance or need professional help, we invite you to contact us for a free consultation. Give us a call at [Your Phone Number] or visit us on our website at [Your Website].

Social media is an amazing way to connect with people and stay at the forefront. Being in the home services field for so long we've had the chance to see the difference a solid social media presence can have on a business. We had an customer who was engaging very little with their social media so their page and growth stood stagnant. After discussing the benefits of staying relevant to your audience, they decided to take on social media with our Contractor Connect Social Platform. Here is their growth in just 60 days of utilizing the platform:

- Facebook reach went up 85.2% from their previous 60 days (this is the number of people that see your posts)
- Facebook engaged users went up 133.3% from their previous 60 days (these are people that performed some action on their post, liked, shared, clicked on)
- Facebook organic impressions went up 148.6% from their previous 60 days (this is the number of times posts were seen)
- Instagram reach went up 39.5% from the previous 60 days
- Instagram impressions went up 19.1% from the previous 60 days

By leveraging these strategies and tailoring your content to each platform, contractors can create a strong social media presence that resonates with their audience and attracts new customers. Regularly analyzing performance metrics and adapting your strategy based on feedback will contribute to ongoing success across all platforms. Social media is a powerful tool that, when used effectively, can significantly boost your business's visibility and growth.

ORGANIC VS PAID SOCIAL ADS FOR HOME SERVICES CONTRACTORS

When deciding between organic marketing and paid social media marketing, you might wonder which is worth your time and investment. Understanding the differences between the two will help you determine the best approach for your business. Let's explore the distinctions between organic and paid social media marketing for home services contractors, including roofers, painters, plumbers, electricians, and handymen.

Organic Social Media

Organic social media refers to all the content you post on your social media profiles without paying for promotion. This content is visible to your followers and anyone who visits your page, but it may not reach a wider audience beyond that. Organic social media is an excellent way to connect with your existing customers and build brand awareness and trust within your community.

Challenges of Organic Social Media:
- Limited Reach: The number of followers who see your posts can vary significantly. Factors include the platform's algorithm, the engagement level of your followers, and the timing of your post.
- Algorithm Impact: Platforms like Facebook and Instagram often show your posts to only a small percentage of your followers. Studies show organic reach on Facebook is around 5.5%, and on Instagram, it's about 6%.

Strategies to Increase Organic Reach:
- Engaging Content: Post engaging content, such as personalized posts of your team or educational videos.
- Use Hashtags: Utilize relevant hashtags to increase visibility.

Paid Social Media

Paid social media involves paying to promote your content to a broader audience. This can include targeted advertisements that appear in users' feeds or sponsored posts that appear at the top of search results. Paid social media can be a powerful tool for reaching new customers and driving traffic to your website.

Benefits of Paid Social Media:
- Expanded Reach: Paid ads allow you to extend your reach beyond your followers. By targeting specific demographics and locations, you can ensure your ads reach the right people.
- Increased Visibility: Paid ads help you stand out. By promoting your content, you can ensure it appears prominently in users' feeds or search results, increasing the likelihood of engagement and conversions.
- Faster Results: While organic social media takes time to grow, paid ads deliver quicker results. Investing in targeted ad campaigns can generate immediate traffic to your website, increase service bookings, and achieve marketing goals faster.
- Tracking and Analytics: Paid social media platforms provide detailed analytics and tracking tools that allow you to measure the effectiveness of your campaigns. You can track metrics like impressions, clicks, conversions, and engagement rates, which allows you to optimize your strategy and make data-driven decisions.

Combining Organic and Paid Strategies

While both organic and paid social media can be effective marketing strategies, they serve different purposes. Organic social media is great for building relationships, sharing information, and fostering trust. Paid social media helps you reach beyond your current audience to find new potential customers and drive traffic to your website, which can also improve your SEO. Using both strategies together creates a well-rounded social media presence that helps you be seen by more potential customers.

Getting Started with Paid Social Ads

Now that you've decided to venture into paid social media marketing, the next step is determining the right type of ad and platform to use. Here are some valuable tips to help you navigate the world of paid ads with confidence and clarity.

Types of Paid Social Media Ads

1. Sponsored Posts: Ads that appear in a user's feed and look like regular social media posts but are labeled "sponsored." These ads can promote events, specials, or new services.
2. Display Ads: Image-based ads that appear on the side or bottom of a user's social media feed. These ads can promote a specific service or product and include a call-to-action button that directs users to your website.
3. Video Ads: Similar to sponsored posts but feature a video instead of an image. These ads can showcase your services, provide educational content, give a tour of your work sites, or offer an introduction to your team.
4. Carousel Ads: Ads that allow you to showcase multiple images or videos within a single ad. This format is great for highlighting different services or projects.
5. Story Ads: Full-screen ads that appear within a user's social media story. These ads can promote your services or products and include interactive elements like polls and quizzes.

By understanding the differences between organic and paid social media marketing and utilizing both effectively, home services contractors can build a robust online presence that attracts and retains customers.

These are just a few examples of the types of paid social media ads available. Each platform offers its unique ad formats and targeting options, so it's important to choose the right type of ad for your specific marketing goals and audience.

YouTube Marketing

Did you know that YouTube ranks as the second most popular search engine, right after Google? Many businesses focus heavily on traditional search engine optimization (SEO) but often overlook the significant opportunities that video marketing can offer. Implementing a video marketing strategy can enhance your online visibility, improve SEO efforts, and boost conversion rates.

Why Use Youtube Video Marketing?
There are several compelling reasons for contractors to use video marketing:
1. Increased Search Engine Exposure: Videos can secure additional placeholders in search engine results for your targeted keywords, increasing your online presence.
2. Enhanced SEO: Videos drive traffic to your website and create relevant links, improving your SEO.
3. Improved Conversion Rates: Videos resonate more deeply with potential customers, encouraging them to take action.

Benefits of Video Marketing

Enhanced SEO Efforts
The other thing that we can accomplish with video is the enhancement of our SEO efforts. By creating good video content, you have the ability to drive inbound links to your website from high level video sites like YouTube and Vimeo.

Again, you don't want to have just the generic Home, About Us, Our Services, Contact Us pages on your website.

You want to have a page for each of your core services and products. Videos that link to those pages is going to help with that SEO effort. Also, you're going to find that video content on your website, and on the pages of your site, actually reduces your bounce rate and increases visitors' time on your site.

These are SEO factors. 'Bounce rate' refers to somebody getting to your page and clicking back immediately or browsing away. Google understands those actions as the page not being relevant to that search.

If the majority of the people that get to your site click off and leave right away, your bounce rate is high, and Google is going to start to show you less prominently in their results. That's part of the Google algorithm. The other factor is the amount of time spent on the site. If somebody gets to your page, stays there for ten seconds, and then moves on, the visit might not get treated like a bounce, but Google is still looking at the length on the site.

If you have a video and a visitor takes the time to watch it in its entirety, that's improving your website visit length statistics. Even if they only watch a couple seconds of the video, you have captured their attention long enough that Google is going to see your site is relevant.

Don't get confused by the notion that having video on your page automatically improves your SEO. That's not necessarily the case. But having people stay on your page longer and not bounce off does impact SEO. Here's an example of how you can drive some links with your videos.

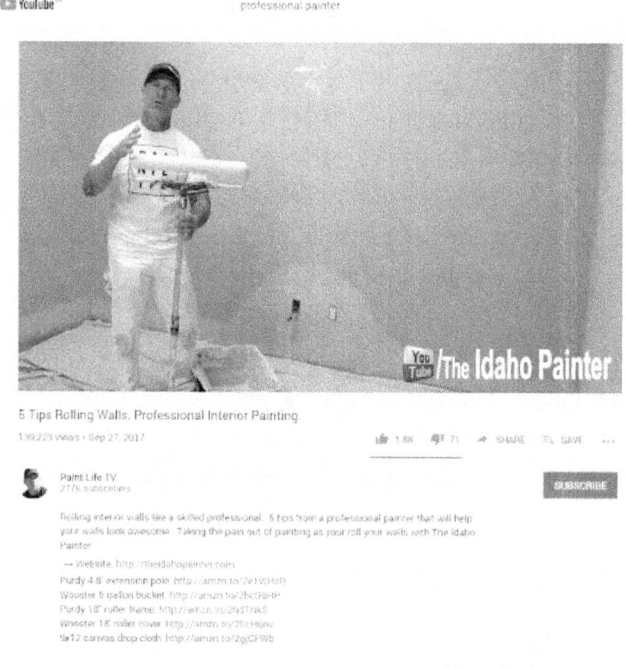

Here's an example of the YouTube channel on "Paint Live TV", which is a professional painting service in Idaho. You can see in the description area that they have included their website link: Idahopainter.com. This link now connects you from YouTube to their site, and that's a relevant high impact link. You can do the same thing. I would suggest that you do not link to the home page, but rather to the specific subpage related to the video, like the interior painting tools or the surface preparation page.

Improved Conversion Rates

Videos can improve conversion rates by engaging visitors more effectively than text alone. When potential customers watch a video of you explaining your services, it builds trust and makes them more likely to choose your business.

Creating Effective Video Content

Types of Videos to Create
1. Introduction Video: Create a brief introductory video for your website. Introduce your business, highlight your services, and invite viewers to contact you.
2. Service-Specific Videos: Make short videos for each of your core services, explaining what you offer and why customers should choose you.
3. Frequently Asked Questions (FAQs): Address common questions in short videos. This helps educate your audience and positions you as an expert in your field.

How to Create Your Videos
You don't need a high-end production crew to create effective videos. With a smartphone or a webcam, you can produce quality content. Keep your videos simple, authentic, and to the point.

Script Example:
"Thank you for visiting [Your Company]'s website. We specialize in [Your Services] in the [Your Area]. Our team is dedicated to providing top-notch service. Contact us today at [Your Phone Number]."

Leveraging Your Video Content

Uploading and Optimizing Videos on YouTube
1. Setup a YouTube Channel: Create a YouTube channel for your business. Use a title that includes your city and service, such as "Denver Roofing Services – XYZ Contractors."
2. Upload Videos: Upload your videos to your channel. Ensure each video is properly titled with relevant keywords, such as "Denver Roof Repair – XYZ Contractors."
3. Optimize Descriptions: Include a link to your website at the beginning of each video description, such as "Visit us online at http://yourcompany.com/roofrepair." Add a brief description of the video content and your services, and include your business's name, ad-

dress, and phone number (NAP) for consistent citations.

Video Tagging Best Practices
- Title: Use keywords that people will search for, like "City + Service – Company Name."
- Description: Start with a clickable link (http://yourwebsite.com), followed by a brief service description. Always include your NAP (Name, Address, Phone Number) information.
- Tags: Use relevant keywords and your company name.

Examples of Successful Contractor Videos

Introduction Video
"Thank you for visiting XYZ Contractors. We specialize in roofing, painting, and plumbing services in the Denver area. Contact us today at 555-5555."

Service-Specific Video
"At XYZ Contractors, we offer top-quality roof repair services in Denver. Whether you need a minor repair or a full roof replacement, our team is here to help. Call us today at 555-5555."

Video marketing is a powerful tool for contractors. It enhances your SEO efforts, improves conversion rates, and helps you connect with potential customers on a deeper level. By creating simple, authentic videos and optimizing them for search engines, you can significantly boost your online visibility and attract more business. Start leveraging the power of video marketing today to take your contracting business to the next level.

Overall, social media channels such as Facebook, Instagram, LinkedIn, and Youtube are powerful tools that allow home services contractors to connect with their customers and community on a more personal level. It helps in building your brand and staying in the forefront of people's minds. Social media also helps build a sense of community.

Embracing social media as part of a comprehensive marketing strategy can lead to improved customer loyalty, a broader reach, and a positive impact on the overall success of your business.

Chapter 11
Leveraging Email Marketing To Connect With Your Customers

Home services contractors canLeverage email marketing to connect with customers on a deeper level, get more reviews, more social media followers and ultimately more repeat AND referral business.

Ever since there's been email, there's been email marketing. Email marketing is one of the oldest forms of advertising your business on the Internet. Although it gets a bad rap because of all the spam going around, it's still one of the most effective forms of marketing.

Email marketing is a powerful way to get instant traffic to your website and getting the phone to ring, but there is a right way and a wrong way to use it.

Did you know the easiest customer to sell to is the customer you already have?

Every self-proclaimed marketing expert will tell you that's nothing new. With that said, many contractors hardly ever market or keep in touch with their existing customer base. Companies will spend thousands of dollars trying to get new customers but never think to market to the customers who already buy from them.

Why is that? I have a lot of ideas about this. I suspect business owners think that once a customer buys from them, they will just keep coming back on their own. Or maybe they simply don't want to bother their customers. The truth is customers want to hear from you and they want to be touched by your business. If you don't, your competition will.

How Do You Start an Email Marketing Campaign?

The first thing you need is an email marketing service. You shouldn't do this yourself for several reasons:
1. Your Internet Service Provider (ISP) will blacklist you for sending bulk mail.
2. You would have no stats for tracking your open emails
3. It would look unprofessional coming from your Microsoft Outlook box

With that said, let's take a look at some of the popular email marketing services, all of which are paid services and are priced based on the amount of emails you send. They all start at around $15.00 per month to send a couple hundred emails.

Constant Contact

I have used Constant Contact in the past and I like it for several reasons. It has great tracking stats, the ability to post to your social networks and a relatively user-friendly interface.

Constant Contact has many templates available for use. You can also add your own custom templates. I think custom templates are a MUST for any business wanting to promote their brand. You will have to know a bit of HTML but if you don't, you can have a web designer create one for you at a fairly inexpensive cost.

MailChimp

Mailchimp is another service I have personally used and recommend. It's relatively easy to use and offers similar features to Constant Contact. The interface is clean and easy to use. Prices start at $14.00.

HubSpot

HubSpot is a comprehensive marketing and sales platform offering robust email marketing tools among its array of features. It is an ideal solution for businesses looking to integrate email marketing with other aspects of their digital strategy, such as customer relationship management (CRM), social media, and content marketing. Hubspot can be pricy but it offers more comprehensive suite of tools as compared to Mailchimp or Constant Contact.

GoHighLevel

GoHighLevel is a versatile platform providing a holistic suite of tools, including email marketing, landing pages, and workflow automations to streamline communication and engagement. It is designed to help businesses manage all their marketing activities from a single platform, enhancing efficiency and effectiveness.

Key Features:

- All-in-One Platform: Manage email marketing, CRM, and more from one place.
- Automation: Automate your email marketing campaigns for better efficiency.
- Analytics: Track and analyze your email marketing performance.
- Templates: Access to a range of customizable email templates.
- Integration: Integrates seamlessly with other tools and platforms.

How to Get Email Addresses

I am asked on a regular basis about how to get email addresses. It's not as easy as sending a letter in the USPS mail to anyone you want to. The reality of it is that just because they are your customer and you have their email address doesn't mean you can send them anything if you don't have their permission.

This certainly is a fine line, because you somehow already have their email address, and they have used your services before, so is it really considered spam? Technically, yes. You didn't ask them if you could send them specials or a newsletter in email form.

The first thing you really want to do is get your customers' permission to add them to your email list. There are a variety of ways to do this, including placing a form on your website, putting a sign-up sheet on your counter or even a putting a space on your job ticket that they sign when you complete your service.

Explain that you send out tips about your industry or specials on a monthly basis and would love to have them on your mailing list. You might even offer a discount coupon off your services if they sign up.

Getting that email address is valuable, so if it cost you 5%, go for it. Remember, you want the opportunity to have your company's name in front of your customers every single month. You want to remain top-of-mind if one of their friends is looking for services like yours or if they run into an emergency.

I had a pest control service provider come to my home several years ago. He did a good job and was very professional.

Four or five years later, I needed the services of the company again. I lost his business card and could not remember the name of the company. I had to find another pest removal service. He lost the business because he never stayed in contact with me. It was a big job that he lost, $1,500.00 to be exact.

Start building your list today.

What to Send and How Often

First, what do I send? You must use the 80/20 rule, 80 percent good information and 20 percent sales. If all you send is emails about what services you offer, no one will ever read it. It's a great way to kill your list.

Draft up some information about your industry, give good homeowner tips, throw in some DIY tips, and make sure it's information that will help your users. For the 20% sales, add a coupon or a special you are having, or offer something for your customers' friends and family.

How often you send your emails is very important. I always go with once per month, around the same time every month.

It is important to commit to a date. More than once a month is too much and annoys people.

I get an email from a company I purchased from in the past and get 3-4 emails a week from them, 100% sales, sometimes several times a day. I HATE IT and it drives me nuts. I removed myself from that list very quickly as I'm sure others have as well.

Get Legal

Make sure you have allowed customers the option to opt-out of receiving email messages at the bottom of every message.

Make sure that it's easy because nothing is more annoying than receiving emails that you don't want. If someone does not want to receive your messages, then remove them from your list.

They may be getting emails from too many sources and just want to clean out their email box. It does not mean they will never buy from you again. But I will tell you this, if they want out and you keep sending email to them, it's a sure-fire way to bother them and they will likely never buy from you again.

Again, you want to leverage email marketing as part of your overall Internet marketing strategy. The best way to use it is to be sure you're collecting the email address from all your customers and prospects.

From there, use email marketing to get online reviews, engagement on your social media accounts and remain top-of-mind as a strategy to get more repeat and referral business.

What is the Best Time to Send an Email Campaign?
These general email send time tips are widely accepted by the email marketing community. They are great when you're starting off, but **be sure to read on and see why they won't always work.**

- **Day-time vs. Night-time:** While this one may be obvious, it's usually better to send out your email campaigns during the daytime. You know, when people are awake. Not asleep.

- **Mad Mondays:** The general consensus is that you should avoid sending out email blasts on Mondays. Why? People are already bummed out about the end of the weekend. They march into the office and are flooded with emails they've collected over the past few days. What's the first thing they do? Delete those emails of course!

- **Weekends:** Historically, weekends are the days when folks are out running errands and going on adventures. Weekends tend to have low open rates, so most marketers avoid them like the plague.

- **Fan Favorites:** Tuesday, Wednesday, and Thursday. Tuesday, Wednesday, and Thursday have traditionally been favorite days to send email campaigns, as email marketers seek to avoid the Monday angst and Friday's itchy feet. MailChimp confirms that Tuesday and Thursday are the two most popular days to send email newsletters.

The Importance of a Monthly Newsletter for Home Service Contractors
In the realm of email marketing for home service contractors, a monthly

newsletter emerges as a cornerstone of customer-engagement marketing. Unlike other forms of communication, a well-crafted newsletter serves as a consistent touch-point, keeping your business at the forefront of your customers' minds and nurturing a relationship that transcends individual service visits.

For contractors offering services such as roofing, painting, plumbing, electrical work, or handyman services, customer visits might be occasional or seasonal. A monthly newsletter acts as a lifeline, bridging the gap between appointments. It ensures that you remain a constant presence in your customers' lives, offering reassurance and valuable insights, even when they don't require immediate services. It's an opportunity to empower them with knowledge, fostering a sense of active participation in maintaining and improving their homes.

Components of an Impactful Monthly Newsletter

Leverage Seasonal Maintenance Tips
Incorporate a strategic approach by aligning your newsletter with various seasonal maintenance tips. For example, provide tips on preparing homes for winter, spring cleaning, summer landscaping, and fall gutter maintenance. Tailor your content to align with these themes, amplifying the relevance and resonance of your messages.

A Dash of DIY: Home Improvement Tips
One of the key components that draw engagement and anticipation is the inclusion of DIY home improvement tips. This not only captures attention but also elevates your newsletter's value. Customers look forward to these practical tips, fostering a sense of well-rounded care beyond professional services.

Celebrating Your Team
Introduce a personal touch by showcasing new team members, celebrating work anniversaries, and acknowledging the accomplishments of your staff. This not only humanizes your business but also creates a sense of community and shared achievement.

New Service Offerings and Training Updates
Keep your customers abreast of the evolving landscape of home services by highlighting new service offerings, detailing relevant training your team has attended, and proudly sharing any awards received. This positions your business at the forefront of innovation and expertise.

The Power of Recognition
Include any accolades or awards your business has earned. Customer trust is often fortified by external validation, and sharing your achievements instills confidence and pride among your audience.

Embrace the opportunity to go beyond transactional interactions, guiding your customers on a journey of holistic home care. Your monthly newsletter is not just a communication tool; it's an extension of the quality service you provide. Let it be a beacon of care, illuminating the path to a well-maintained home for every subscriber who opens their inbox to your words.

Other Ways to Use Email Marketing
While a monthly newsletter is a powerful tool, you can further leverage email marketing for a myriad of impactful engagements. Promote your social media channels, encouraging subscribers to connect with your business on various platforms for a more interactive experience. Don't shy away from seeking reviews – ask satisfied customers to share their positive experiences on Google and other review platforms, fortifying your online reputation. Share exclusive home maintenance tips, sneak peeks into upcoming services, or even spotlight customer success stories.

The versatility of email marketing extends beyond the routine, offering you a dynamic platform to nurture customer relationships, boost engagement, and foster a vibrant community of homeowners. Email marketing is not just a strategy; it's a conduit for service, education, and enduring connections. Embrace it, Home Service Contractors, and witness the transformative impact it brings to your business and the lives you touch.

Chapter 12

Leveraging Awards to Position Yourself as the #1 Contractor in Your Area

Why Pursue Awards?
Awards and recognitions can significantly enhance the reputation and credibility of home services contractors. They serve as third-party endorsements, validating the quality of your work and business practices. They also signal to potential customers that your services are trustworthy and reliable.

Awards can set you apart from competitors. When customers see that you've received accolades, they're more likely to choose your services over those of unrecognized competitors. Being recognized for excellence can also boost employee morale and motivation, fostering a culture of pride and dedication within your team.

Moreover, awards provide excellent content for marketing materials, including your website, social media, and advertising campaigns. They offer compelling reasons for customers to choose your services. Lastly, winning awards often involves media coverage and public recognition, increasing your visibility in the community and beyond.

Notable Awards for Home Services Contractors
Here is a comprehensive list of awards that home services contractors can pursue, along with details on how to apply for them:

Industry-Specific Awards:

Angie's List Super Service Award:
- Criteria: Maintain an "A" rating overall, pass a background check, and be in good standing with Angie's List.
- Application Process: Ensure your business profile is updated and encourage satisfied customers to leave positive reviews on Angie's List.

HomeAdvisor's Best of HomeAdvisor Award:
- Criteria: Maintain a high average rating, have a minimum number of reviews, and be an active member of HomeAdvisor.
- Application Process: Actively manage your HomeAdvisor profile, solicit reviews from customers, and maintain high ratings.

Houzz Best of Houzz Award:
- Criteria: Based on the popularity of your projects among Houzz users and maintaining high customer satisfaction.
- Application Process: Keep your Houzz profile updated with high-quality photos of your work and encourage customers to leave reviews.

GuildQuality Guildmaster Award:
- Criteria: Achieve a high customer recommendation rate as measured by GuildQuality.
- Application Process: Join GuildQuality, conduct surveys with your customers, and maintain high satisfaction ratings.

NARI (National Association of the Remodeling Industry) Contractor of the Year (CotY) Awards:
- Criteria: Excellence in remodeling projects across various categories.
- Application Process: Submit detailed project descriptions, photos, and customer testimonials through the NARI website.

The Remodeling 550:
- Criteria: Be one of the largest and most successful remodeling companies in the U.S. based on revenue growth.
- Application Process: Complete the survey provided by Remodeling Magazine detailing your business performance.

Local and Regional Awards:

1. Local Chamber of Commerce Awards: Varies by chamber but typically includes business excellence and community involvement. Nominate your business through your local chamber of commerce website or by attending chamber events.
2. Better Business Bureau (BBB) Torch Awards: Demonstrate ethical practices and community involvement. Nominate your business through the BBB website and provide supporting documentation.
3. Local Home Show Awards: Best booth, best demonstration, and best overall presentation at local home shows. Participate in local home shows and ensure your booth is engaging and professionally presented.

National and International Awards:
1. Inc. 5000: Fastest-growing private companies in the U.S. based on revenue growth over a three-year period. Submit financial performance data through the Inc. 5000 application portal.
2. Entrepreneur 360: Best entrepreneurial companies based on innovation, growth, leadership, and impact. Complete the application form detailing your business performance and strategies.
3. Good Housekeeping Seal: Products that pass rigorous testing by the Good Housekeeping Institute. Submit your products for evaluation

through the Good Housekeeping website.

Specialized Awards:
1. Green Builder Media's Green Home of the Year Awards: Excellence in sustainable home building and remodeling. Submit project descriptions, photos, and sustainability metrics through the Green Builder Media website.
2. National Roofing Contractors Association (NRCA) Awards: Outstanding roofing projects and contractors. Submit detailed project descriptions, photos, and customer testimonials through the NRCA website.

Leveraging Awards in Your Marketing
Once you've earned awards and recognitions, it's crucial to leverage them effectively in your marketing efforts. Here are some strategies to maximize the impact:

Website Home Page:
- Feature your awards prominently on your website's home page. Use badges, logos, and a dedicated section highlighting your achievements.

Social Media Banners and Posts:
- Update your social media banners to include award logos and announcements. Create engaging posts celebrating your achievements and thanking your customers for their support.

Press Releases:
- Issue a press release announcing your award wins. Press releases get sent out via presswire to local media outlets like your local NBC, ABC, CBS stations, radio stations, and newspapers.

Email Marketing:
- Include award announcements in your email newsletters. Highlight how these recognitions set you apart and reinforce your commitment to excellence.

Customer Communications:
- Mention your awards in customer communications, such as email signatures, invoices, and thank-you notes.

Marketing Collateral:
- Add award logos and mentions to your brochures, business cards, and other marketing materials.

Community Involvement:
- Share your achievements at community events, local meetings, and industry gatherings. Use these opportunities to build relationships and enhance your reputation.

Pursuing and winning awards can significantly elevate your status as the go-to home services contractor in your area. By understanding the available awards, effectively applying for them, and leveraging the recognition in your marketing efforts, you can build a strong reputation, attract more customers, and grow your business. Embrace these opportunities and watch your business thrive as you become a recognized leader in the home services industry.

Chapter 13

Your Journey to Becoming the #1 Home Services Contractor in Your Area

As you embark on your journey to become the top contractor in your area, it's essential to recognize the importance of a comprehensive and well-rounded marketing strategy. This book has guided you through various facets of effective marketing, each playing a crucial role in your overall success. Let's reflect on the key takeaways from each chapter and how they collectively contribute to positioning you as the go-to contractor in your region.

Laying the Foundation of Successful Marketing
Every great marketing strategy begins with a solid foundation. In Chapter 1, we discussed the importance of understanding your target market, defining your unique selling proposition (USP), and setting clear, achievable goals. These elements serve as the bedrock upon which your entire marketing strategy is built. Knowing who you are, what you offer, and whom you serve allows you to tailor your marketing efforts to attract the right customers.

Evaluating and Transforming Your Marketing Approach
In Chapter 2, we delved into the necessity of evaluating your current marketing efforts and making necessary transformations. By conducting

a thorough analysis of your existing strategies, you can identify what's working and what needs improvement. Embracing change and being willing to adapt are crucial for staying ahead in a competitive market.

How Homeowners Choose a Contractor

Understanding your customers' decision-making process is vital. Chapter 3 explored the factors that influence homeowners when choosing a contractor. Trust, reputation, and evidence of quality work are paramount. By aligning your marketing messages with these factors, you can better appeal to potential customers and address their primary concerns.

Your Website: Position Yourself as the Pro

Your website is often the first impression potential customers have of your business. In Chapter 4, we emphasized the importance of a professional, user-friendly website. It should not only showcase your services but also position you as an expert in your field. High-quality content, easy navigation, and strong calls to action are essential components of an effective website.

Local SEO: Understanding the Elements

Chapter 5 highlighted the significance of local SEO in driving traffic to your website. Optimizing your online presence for local searches ensures that your business appears in search results when homeowners in your area look for contractors. This includes optimizing your Google My Business profile, gathering positive reviews, and ensuring your website is mobile-friendly.

Your Online Reputation & Why It Matters

Your reputation can make or break your business. Chapter 6 discussed the impact of online reviews and how they influence potential customers' perceptions. Actively managing your online reputation by encouraging satisfied customers to leave positive reviews and promptly addressing any negative feedback is crucial for building trust and credibility.

Overview of Paid Online Advertising Opportunities

In Chapter 7, we explored various paid online advertising opportunities.

From Google Ads to social media advertising, these platforms can help you reach a broader audience and drive targeted traffic to your website. Understanding the different options and how to leverage them effectively can significantly enhance your marketing efforts.

Pay Per Click for Home Services Contractors
Chapter 8 delved deeper into pay-per-click (PPC) advertising, a powerful tool for generating leads and driving immediate traffic to your website. By creating well-structured campaigns, targeting the right keywords, and continually optimizing your ads, you can maximize the return on your PPC investment.

Paid Online Directories - Which Ones Should You Consider Advertising In?
In Chapter 9, we discussed the importance of paid online directories. Listings on sites like Yelp, Yellow Pages, and the Better Business Bureau can increase your visibility and credibility. Carefully selecting the directories that align with your target market and investing in premium placements can enhance your online presence.

Social Media Mastery
Social media platforms offer unique opportunities to connect with your audience. Chapter 10 covered the strategies for mastering social media, from creating engaging content to interacting with your followers. Building a strong social media presence helps you stay top-of-mind and fosters a community around your brand.

Email Marketing to Connect With Your Customers
Email marketing remains a powerful tool for nurturing relationships with your customers. In Chapter 11, we highlighted the importance of regular communication through newsletters, promotions, and personalized messages. By staying in touch with your audience, you can drive repeat business and maintain customer loyalty.

Leveraging Awards to Position Yourself as the #1 Contractor in Your Area

Awards and recognitions can significantly boost your credibility and set you apart from the competition. Chapter 12 explored various awards available to home services contractors and provided insights on how to apply for them. Showcasing these accolades on your website, social media, and marketing materials reinforces your position as a trusted expert in your field.

Bringing It All Together
Your journey to becoming the #1 contractor in your area is an ongoing process that requires dedication, adaptability, and a comprehensive marketing strategy. By laying a strong foundation, continuously evaluating and refining your approach, and leveraging the various tools and tactics discussed in this book, you can build a robust and successful business.

Remember, your success is built on the trust and satisfaction of your customers. Every interaction, from your website and social media presence to your email communications and customer service, contributes to your reputation. Stay committed to delivering exceptional service, continually seek opportunities for improvement, and never stop promoting the unique value you bring to your customers.

As you apply the lessons from each chapter, you'll find yourself well-equipped to navigate the competitive landscape of home services contracting. Your dedication to excellence, combined with a strategic marketing approach, will position you as the go-to contractor in your area, driving growth and success for your business.

If you've gotten to this point and feel like you need some extra help to implement these ideas, Nail It Marketing Pros is here to support you. You can call us directly at 888-857-9548 with any questions that you might have.

Our team will review your entire online marketing effort (Website, Competition, Search Engine Placement, Social Media, etc.) and come back to you with a complete assessment of how you can improve and what you can do to take your online marketing efforts to the next level.

Request A Free Custom Online Marketing Evaluation Now

Your Custom-Tailored Optimization Audit will:

- [ ] Identify key issues that could be harming your website without you even knowing it.

- [ ] Look at where your website stands compared to your competitors.

- [ ] Determine whether SEO is the appropriate route for you to take.

- [ ] Uncover hidden revenue that you're leaving on the table.

- [ ] Offer recommendations that you can put to use immediately

Schedule your custom audit at https://nailitmarketing.agency/marketing-meeting or scan the QR code below to get access to our calendar.

Stay tuned for more Marketing Guides and Resources from Nail It Marketing Pros

Make sure to follow us on Facebook and Instagram for real time updates.

@nailitmarketingpros

Visit us online at:

www.nailitmarketingpros.com

OUR AWARDS & MEDIA SPOTLIGHTS

READY FOR MORE PROJECTS? (888) 857-9548

www.ingramcontent.com/pod-product-compliance
Lightning Source LLC
Chambersburg PA
CBHW071937210526
45479CB00002B/713